Where Was the Room Where It Happened?

The Unofficial
Hamilton: An American Musical
Location Guide

Expanded Edition

Bryan Barreras

with contributions from

Nicole Scholet

This book is dedicated to my wonderful wife, Rebecca, and to my great kids, London and Andrew, who may actually love Hamilton *more than I do. I couldn't have done this without their support.*

TABLE OF CONTENTS*

* Locations marked with an asterisk are new for the expanded edition.

ABOUT THIS BOOK

This book's primary purpose is to provide additional information about the locations that are used and/or mentioned in *Hamilton: An American Musical*. This is made somewhat difficult by the fact that Lin-Manuel Miranda, in crafting what my family and I think is the greatest Broadway show ever, creates scenes for the show that did not take place where he sets them and/or involve characters that did not actually take part in those scenes (and often both). This is not to in any way criticize the historical accuracy of the material, but rather to recognize the difficulty in portraying historical events in an entertaining show (and you can only make so many sets and have so many characters - Miranda acknowledges in *Hamilton - The Revolution* that he deviates from what really happened where necessary for the show's content and flow). I have made a conscious decision to NOT point out historical inaccuracies, because the show could not possibly be better, so all liberties taken by Miranda were justified. If you want to get all the facts, read Ron Chernow's biography, *Alexander Hamilton*, as Miranda did (and as I did) – a tremendous piece of work.

Given the above, I have tried to explain how each location is used in *Hamilton*, either as a setting for a scene, as the location where an event actually occurred, or just mentioned (but is important). Hopefully, you have had or will have the opportunity to see the show and can use this book as a resource to help you appreciate where all the events happened, or as a guide to visit some of these locations to walk in the footsteps of the great men (and women) that helped shape our country.

Because Hamilton has been such a positive experience for me and my family, a portion of profits from sales of this book will be donated to charity. As of the date of this expanded edition, we have donated over $20,000 of book profits to charity, mostly split between **Graham Windham**, the orphanage that Eliza Hamilton started (yes – it still exists!), **HeForShe**, in part because the beat-box that Emma Watson did with Miranda was amazing (it's also a great cause, and my daughter loves Emma Watson), the **National Park Foundation**, because the National Parks have been such a great partner, carrying the book in multiple locations, and **Flamboyan Arts Fund**, which is the organization that benefited from performances of *Hamilton* in Puerto Rico in 2019. We appreciate all the sales that have made this possible.

 @wwtrwih

HOW THIS BOOK WORKS

I have tried to make this book as straightforward as possible, but a few things would benefit from explanation. I use a few different descriptions when referring to the songs and locations, with the following meanings:

- **Setting for** – this means the location is the stage setting in the show for the song;

- **Mentioned in** – this means the location is mentioned in the song, either by name or by referring to something that happened at the location;

- **Location for** – this means the events portrayed in the song happened in real life at the location (even though the stage setting may be different); this occurs most often where a song portrays events that happened in multiple locations at multiple times;

- **Who was *really* there?** – this refers to which historical figures from the show were ever at that location in real life (as best as I could determine based on research). This does not refer to who is portrayed in the show as being there, or to which characters sing any particular song – you can get that information from the *Hamilton* Broadway cast recording (which you own, of course);

Can you go? – this simply means whether the location stills exists in some form that might make it worth your while to see, or whether it has been built over in the ensuing years.

HOW THE MAPS WORK

Most of the locations mentioned in this book include a local map to help you find the location. Because many of the sites are close together, most of the maps include multiple sites, such as the following example (which is the map for Independence Hall):

All of the sites included in this book are indicated with a red star, except for the site that is being discussed, which has a *Hamilton* gold star (which is slightly larger than the red stars). Apologies for the small size of the maps, but I have to balance the content to include as much information as I can in the book.

I would love any input on the book - please send suggestions or comments (e.g., locations to add, thoughts re: connections to the Broadway show) to Info@wwtrwih.com, or tweet suggestions and include @wwtrwih. **Please also see page 160 for info on customizing the book for corporate gifts or event – they make great gifts and swag bag stuffers.**

If you like this book, it would mean a lot to me if you would share it on social media on Facebook, Instagram, Twitter, etc. – please include @wwtrwih and #Hamilton.

ENJOY!

CHAPTER ONE

HAMILTON LOCATIONS
IN NEW YORK CITY

History is happening in Manhattan...

Alexander Hamilton was a New Yorker, so a lot of the events depicted in the show occurred in New York City (and I live in New York City). While this was initially the focus of this book (this book is primarily designed to be a guide for people to see all the locations related to *Hamilton: An American Musical* and to provide historical information about those locations, many of which are in New York City), this expanded edition is in recognition of the fact that not everything happens in New York City.

FRAUNCES TAVERN

Setting for: *Aaron Burr, Sir – Act I*
My Shot – Act I
The Story of Tonight – Act I
The Story of Tonight (Reprise) – Act I
Wait For It – Act I

The tavern is the setting for Aaron Burr, Sir *and* My Shot *(from "Hamilton – The Revolution"), and while it is unclear whether the other songs listed above are also meant to be set in Fraunces Tavern, they each take place in a tavern with a similar set design.*

Who was *really* there? Aaron Burr
Alexander Hamilton
Hercules Mulligan
George Washington

Location: 54 Pearl Street

Subway: ❶ South Ferry; ❷ ❸ Wall Street;
❹ ❺ Bowling Green; Ⓙ Ⓩ Broad Street;
Ⓡ Whitehall Street/South Ferry

Can you go? Yes. It still exists as a national historic landmark, museum and restaurant. The restaurant is open 7 days a week from 11AM-2AM (you can book a table at frauncestavern.com or by calling 212-968-1776). The museum is open 12-5 M-F and 11-5 Sat/Sun. Don't miss the annual Fourth of July early morning walking tour (frauncestavernmuseum.org)!

Designations: New York City Landmark (1965)
National Register of Historic Places (2008)

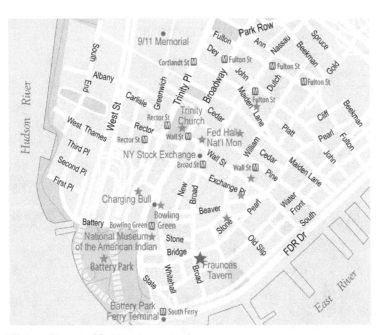

History/Items of Interest:

The structure was built as a house by Etienne DeLancey in 1719 and then sold in 1762 to Samuel Fraunces, who converted it into a tavern named the Queen's Head.

The tavern served as the meeting place of the Sons of Liberty before the Revolution. The New York Chamber of Commerce was founded in 1768 at a meeting here, and the tavern hosted British-American Board of Inquiry meetings during the American Revolution. *Hercules Mulligan* lived on Pearl Street nearby and was a regular at the tavern. The tavern was the site of the dinner held on December 4, 1783 where *George Washington* bade farewell to his Continental Army officers. After the war, the departments of Foreign Affairs, War and Treasury of the Confederation Congress kept their offices here.

The Society of the Cincinnati met at the tavern at least once in the early 1800s – *Aaron Burr* and *Alexander Hamilton* attended. The building was destroyed by fires and rebuilt several times during the 19th century – the original design is unknown. The building passed between several owners and was finally scheduled for demolition in 1900. The Daughters of the American Revolution, among other groups, convinced the New York state government to designate the building as a park, thus saving the building until it was ultimately acquired by the Sons of the Revolution of New York in 1904. The building was "restored" soon thereafter, but without the original plans the restoration is thought to have involved substantial guesswork.

THE COMMON

Setting for: *The Schuyler Sisters – Act I*
Farmer Refuted – Act I

Angelica, Eliza and Peggy work it downtown in the Common in The Schuyler Sisters, *and Alexander Hamilton takes on a pro-British speaker there in* Farmer Refuted.

Who was *really* there?
Aaron Burr
Alexander Hamilton
George Washington

Location: City Hall Park, as this site is now known (bordered by Broadway, Chambers Street and Park Row).

Subway: ❷ ❸ Park Place; ❹ ❺ ❻ Brooklyn Bridge – City Hall; Ⓐ Ⓒ Ⓙ Ⓩ Chambers Street; Ⓡ City Hall

Can you go? Yes. City Hall Park is a great green space in Lower Manhattan that provides a place to relax and take a breath during your day. A stone circular tablet at the southern end of the park provides some history about the site. The park is open from 6AM to midnight.

Designations: New York City Landmark (City Hall)
National Register of Historic Places (City Hall)
National Historic Landmark (City Hall)

History/Items of Interest:

The park's western boundary was a Native American trail that later became Broadway. In 1765, New Yorkers protested the Stamp Act at the site, and a year later the first "Liberty Pole," a mast topped by a vane with the word "liberty," was built at the site (a replica stands between City Hall and Broadway, near its original location).

The Common was the site of *Alexander Hamilton*'s first major public speech, at a meeting of the Sons of Liberty on July 6, 1774, where he spoke in support of the Boston Tea Party and a boycott of British goods. When Hamilton (with others) stole cannons from Ft. George in The Battery on August 23, 1775, they brought the cannons to the Common. On July 9, 1776, *George Washington* read the Declaration of Independence to a crowd at the Common.

During the American Revolution, the British controlled New York and used the debtor's prison on the north end of the Common (where the Tweed Courthouse now stands) to hold prisoners, executing 250 of them on gallows behind the Soldiers' Barracks.

New Yorkers used the park for gatherings throughout the 19th century, including meetings after the declaration of the Mexican-American War in 1846, and a call to volunteers in 1862 to enlist in the Civil War (during the Civil War the park was used to house troops). After President Lincoln was assassinated, his funeral procession for New York residents began at City Hall.

The park is home to more than a dozen monuments and the Mould fountain in the center of the park. In 1991, during the construction of a nearby federal office building, an African burial ground was uncovered on portions of the northern part of the park.

16

THE BATTERY

East Coast Memorial in The Battery

Mentioned in: *Right Hand Man – Act I*

Some of the battles mentioned in this song were fought at The Battery. This was also the location of Fort George, where Alexander Hamilton stole British cannons.

Who was *really* there?
Alexander Hamilton
George Washington

Location: Southern tip of Manhattan

Subway: 🅠 South Ferry; ④ ⑤ Bowling Green
🆁 Whitehall Street/South Ferry

Can you go? Yes and no. You can visit and walk around Battery Park (and catch a ferry to the Statue of Liberty or Ellis Island there), but you'll mainly be visiting a part of the city that didn't exist in the 1800s (see "History"). You can also visit the Alexander Hamilton U.S. Custom House, which sits where Fort George was located.

Designations: New York City Landmark
National Register of Historic Places

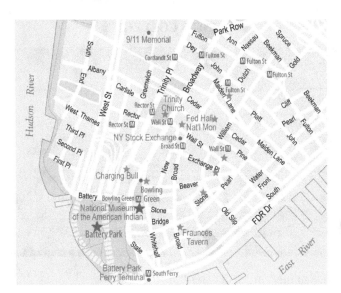

History/Items of Interest:

The southern tip of Manhattan has been known as The Battery since the Dutch settled the island and constructed Fort Amsterdam there in the 17th century to protect the city from approaches by sea.

Fort Amsterdam changed names several times (based upon the ruling country), including being named Fort George during the rule of George I, George II and George III. During the American Revolution, *George Washington*'s troops seized the fort from the British in 1775. Guns from the fort fired on the British during the Battle of Long Island. *Alexander Hamilton* (along with several of his fellow King's College students) stole cannons from Fort George on August 23, 1775. The British recaptured Fort George and ruled New York from the fort for the remainder of the Revolution. The colonists finally took back the fort on Evacuation Day on November 25, 1783 after the British left.

Fort George was torn down in 1790, and its materials were used as landfill for the area that became Battery Park. While Fort George had been located on the shoreline, the Alexander Hamilton U.S. Custom House (which sits where Fort George was located) is now several blocks from shore due to landfilling over the years.

The West Battery (now called Castle Clinton) was built in 1811 in The Battery when it was determined that fortifications in the area were still needed due to further conflicts with the British in the War of 1812. Castle Clinton was originally built on an island off the shore, but now sits within Battery Park due to landfilling.

Battery Park was renamed as The Battery by the New York City Department of Parks and the Battery Conservancy in 2015.

KING'S COLLEGE

College Hall at King's College, 1790

Mentioned in: *My Shot – Act I*
Blow Us All Away – Act II

Alexander Hamilton sings about getting a scholarship to King's College in My Shot*, and Philip Hamilton has just graduated from the college in* Blow Us All Away.

Who was *really* there? Alexander Hamilton
Philip Hamilton

Location: King's College was bordered by present-day West Broadway, Murray Street, Barclay Street and Church Street.

Subway: Historic Site of King's College:
① ② ③ Ⓐ Ⓒ Ⓙ Ⓩ Chambers Street
④ ⑤ ⑥ Brooklyn Bridge – City Hall
Ⓡ City Hall

Columbia University:
① 116th St. – Columbia University

Can you go? No and yes. King's College is now known as Columbia College, the oldest undergraduate college at Columbia University, which is located on the Upper West Side in Manhattan – the main entrance is on Broadway at 116th Street. Groups of fewer than ten people can tour Columbia's Morningside campus on their own or join a guided tour at 1PM M-F (the Visitors Center is open 9-5 M-F; you can get a self-guided tour there, which tells you where to find statues of Hamilton and Thomas Jefferson).

History/Items of Interest:

King's College was founded by royal charter of King George II and enrolled its first class in a room in Trinity Church in 1754. The land for the Park Place location (where *Alexander Hamilton* attended) was presented to the college by Trinity Church. John Jay (*Federalist Papers* author) also graduated from the college.

When the American Revolution began, the president was Myles Cooper (a royalist) – Cooper was threatened and ultimately chased back to England by a mob of patriots in May 1775. Hamilton held off the mob long enough for Cooper to escape by doing what he did best, launching into a speech (condemning the mob's conduct).

The campus was used as a military hospital during the war, first by the Continental Army and then by the British after they seized New York in late 1776 (until they vacated the city in 1783).

The college reopened in 1784 (largely due to the efforts of Hamilton and Jay) under a New York State charter as Columbia College. A charter from New York City in 1787 established Columbia College in its present form (and remains in force today, with slight amendments).

The college was renamed Columbia University in 1896, with the undergraduate school keeping the name Columbia College. The campus relocated to its current Upper West Side location in 1897.

Hamilton Hall is an academic building on the Columbia campus, and a statue of Alexander Hamilton stands outside the building entrance. Appropriately given its namesake, Hamilton Hall has been the site for much student protest activity over the years.

RICHMOND HILL

Location for: *Right Hand Man – Act I*
Your Obedient Servant – Act II

Aaron Burr met George Washington in Washington's office at Richmond Hill during the American Revolution, and this meeting occurs in Right Hand Man. *Burr later lived at Richmond Hill when he exchanged letters with Alexander Hamilton about their fateful duel as sung in* Your Obedient Servant.

Who was *really* there?
John Adams
Aaron Burr
Alexander Hamilton
James Madison
George Washington

Location: Present-day Varick Street, between Charlton Street and Vandam Street.

Subway: ❶ Houston Street
ⓒ ⓔ Spring Street

Can you go? Not really – you can visit the neighborhood where Richmond Hill was once located (a portion of which has been designated a landmark and a historic district), but the house itself no longer exists.

Designations: New York City Landmark (1966)
National Register of Historic Places (1973)

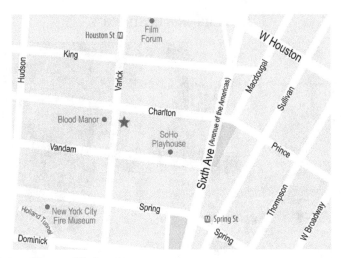

History/Items of Interest:

Richmond Hill was built on a 26-acre parcel of land just south of modern-day Greenwich Village and served as the residence/office of several of the major names of Revolutionary America.

First was *George Washington* – Richmond Hill served as his headquarters from April 1776 until the British forced the retreat of the Continental Army in August 1776 (after the Battle of Long Island) – it was here that he met *Aaron Burr*. The British occupied the property for the remainder of the war.

Next was *John Adams* – he and Abigail Adams lived there during his tenure as vice president under Washington while the nation's capital was in New York City.

Finally, the property was purchased in 1794 by Burr, who lived there with his daughter, Theodosia. Burr used the mansion to entertain distinguished guests, including *James Madison*. Burr was living at Richmond Hill at the time of his duel with *Alexander Hamilton*. The property was ultimately seized by Burr's creditors and sold to John Jacob Astor, who developed the property into hundreds of individual lots (Burr actually mapped out the different lots during his ownership, but didn't have the capital to develop them). The house itself was moved and saw several different uses over the years until it was finally demolished in 1849.

A portion of the estate became what is now the Charlton-King-Vandam Historic District (encompassing most of Charlton Street, King Street and Vandam Street between Varick Street and Avenue of the Americas). The district was designated a New York City landmark in 1966 for its concentration of Federal-style row houses and Greek Revival houses.

JEFFERSON'S RESIDENCE

Plaza in front of 59 Maiden Lane

Setting for: *The Room Where It Happens – Act II*

Thomas Jefferson arranged "the meeting...the venue, the menu, the seating" at his residence on Maiden Lane, where he, Alexander Hamilton and James Madison reached a compromise regarding Hamilton's plan to have the federal government assume the debts of the individual states and the permanent location of the nation's capital.

Who was *really* there?   Alexander Hamilton
Thomas Jefferson
James Madison

Location: 57 Maiden Lane

Subway: ② ③ ④ ⑤ Fulton Street
Ⓐ Ⓒ Ⓙ Ⓩ Fulton Street
Ⓡ Cortlandt Street

Can you go?   No and yes. There is a lovely plaza in front of 59 Maiden Lane (57 Maiden Lane no longer exists) where you can relax for a bit during your day, and don't miss the plaque on the outer wall of the building (at the west end of the plaza) commemorating Jefferson's former residence.

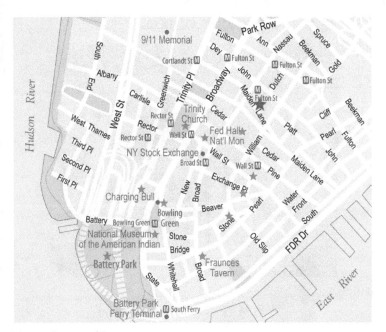

History/Items of Interest:

As recounted by **Thomas Jefferson** (then Secretary of State), *Alexander Hamilton* "basically begged me to join the fray" and to intervene in discussions and negotiations over Hamilton's Report on the Public Credit, which contained a provision that had the federal government assuming the debt of the individual states (and which had twice failed to pass the House of Representatives). Jefferson arranged a meeting among the two of them and *James Madison* (then a highly influential member of the House of Representatives) at Jefferson's residence on or about June 20, 1790. As an aside, Hamilton's Report is on display at the Museum of American Finance on Wall Street (in a room dedicated to Hamilton).

The result of the discussions among the three men was an agreement that Madison would not oppose the bill as strenuously when next brought before the House (by way of amendment from the Senate). In return, it was agreed that the nation's capital should be relocated from New York temporarily to Philadelphia (which was key in convincing the Pennsylvania delegation to go along with the bill) and then ultimately to its current location on the Potomac River. These compromises were borne out through the subsequent passage of the Assumption Bill and the Residence Act of 1790, giving Hamilton the ability to say "[I] got more than [I] gave, and I wanted what I got" (even though the compromise was not popular with many New Yorkers).

FEDERAL HALL

Setting for: *Non-Stop – Act I*
What'd I Miss – Act II
Cabinet Battle #1 – Act II

The murder trial of Levi Weeks, who was defended by Aaron Burr and Alexander Hamilton and which is mentioned in Non-Stop, *was held in City Hall. It was also the first U.S. Capitol Building and would have been the location for debates regarding Hamilton's debt plan in* Cabinet Battle #1, *and the initial meeting between Thomas Jefferson and James Madison when Jefferson first arrived in New York in* What'd I Miss *could have happened here.*

Who was *really* there?	Aaron Burr Alexander Hamilton Thomas Jefferson James Madison George Washington
Location:	26 Wall Street
Subway:	**①** **Ⓡ** Rector Street; **②** **③** **④** **⑤** Wall Street; **Ⓙ** **Ⓩ** Broad Street
Can you go?	Yes. Federal Hall National Memorial (located on the site of the original Federal Hall) is open 9-5 M-F, and the National Park Service announced that the building would be open Saturdays for the summer of 2016. Admission is free.
Designations:	National Memorial (1955) National Register of Historic Places (1966) New York City Landmark (1965)

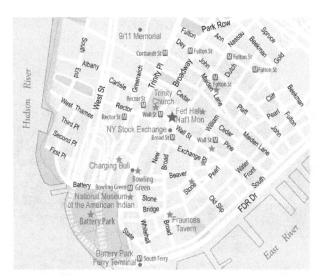

History/Items of Interest:

The original building was built in 1700 as New York's City Hall and housed the Continental Congress following the American Revolution (1785-1789). The building was enlarged and renamed Federal Hall when it became the nation's first Capitol under the new Constitution in 1789, and Congress held their initial meeting there on March 4, 1789. *George Washington* took his oath as the first U.S. president on the building's balcony on April 30, 1789.

Federal Hall initially housed all the branches of the government – the Senate, the House of Representatives (including *James Madison*), the Supreme Court and the Executive Branch offices (Washington and his cabinet, including *Thomas Jefferson*).

The National Park Service calls Federal Hall "the birthplace of American Government," and it lives up to this label. Federal Hall was the site of the Stamp Act Congress in 1765 (which claimed basic rights from *King George III*), and saw the proposal of the Bill of Rights, the drafting of a dozen Constitutional amendments, and the establishment of the U.S. federal court system.

After the government moved to Philadelphia in 1790, the building again housed the New York City government until it was razed in 1812. During this time, the building housed the courtroom where *Aaron Burr* and *Alexander Hamilton* defended their client Levi Weeks from a murder charge in 1800.

The current structure was built in 1842 as the first Customs House. It was designated as Federal Hall National Memorial in 1939. Congress convened in the building in September 2002 (the first time since 1790) to show support for New York following 9/11.

THE GRANGE

Setting for: *Blow Us All Away – Act II*
It's Quiet Uptown – Act II
Best of Wives and Best of Women – Act II
Who Lives, Who Dies, Who Tells Your Story – Act II

The Hamiltons were living on the property where the Grange was to be located (the home was still under construction) when Philip Hamilton was killed in his duel – Alexander Hamilton speaks with Philip before his duel in Blow Us All Away, *and Hamilton and Eliza would have taken solace there as sung in* It's Quiet Uptown. *Eliza would have been at the Grange the morning of Hamilton's duel with Aaron Burr and would have spoken to him there in* Best of Wives and Best of Women. *Eliza lived at the Grange for a time after Hamilton's death while she started working on telling his story in* Who Lives, Who Dies, Who Tells Your Story.

Who was *really* there?	Alexander Hamilton Eliza Hamilton
Location:	414 West 141st Street in St. Nicholas Park
Subway:	❶ 137th Street – City College Ⓐ Ⓑ Ⓒ 135th Street
Can you go?	Yes. Hamilton Grange National Memorial is operated by the National Park Service and has ranger-led tours. The memorial is open 9-5 W-Sun, and admission is free.
Designations:	National Memorial (1962) National Historic Landmark (1960) National Register of Historic Places (1966)

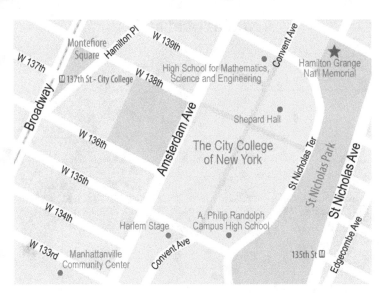

History/Items of Interest:

Alexander Hamilton bought the property that would eventually house the Grange in 1800, and the home was completed in 1802. Hamilton hired John McComb, Jr. as the architect for the home, and Ezra Weeks was the primary contractor (the brother of Levi Weeks, mentioned in *Non-Stop* as being the defendant in the murder trial with *Aaron Burr* and Hamilton as co-counsel).

Hamilton named it the Grange after his grandfather's estate in Scotland, and it was the only home ever owned by Hamilton (as well as the only residence of his that survives to this day). He lived there with *Eliza Hamilton* and the rest of his family. While *Philip Hamilton* lived on the property (the family lived in an existing building on the property while the Grange was being built), the home was completed after his death in the duel with George Eacker in November 1801. The home provided Hamilton with a retreat from the bustle on his downtown law practice to spend time with Eliza and their children, while also giving him and Eliza a place to host parties and socialize (including hosting a ball for 70+ guests just a couple of months before his duel with Burr).

After Eliza sold the property in 1833, the home was moved twice. It was acquired by St. Luke's Episcopal Church in the late 1800s and moved to present-day Convent Avenue. The American Scenic and Historic Preservation Society bought the building and turned it into a museum in 1924. It was transferred to the National Park Service and authorized as a National Memorial by Congress in 1962, and after a long period of disuse and then renovation (to restore the appearance to when Hamilton lived there) and relocation, the Grange was re-opened to the public in September 2011.

TRINITY CHURCH

Mentioned in: *Who Lives, Who Dies, Who Tells Your Story – Act II*

Eliza Hamilton sings that Angelica Church is buried in Trinity Church near Alexander Hamilton.

Who was *really* there?	Aaron Burr Eliza Hamilton Thomas Jefferson Hercules Mulligan George Washington	Alexander Hamilton Philip Hamilton James Madison Angelica Schuyler
Location:	75 Broadway (Trinity Church); 74 Trinity Place (Trinity Church Cemetery)	
Subway:	① ⓡ Rector Street; ② ③ ④ ⑤ Wall Street; ⓙ ⓩ Broad Street	
Can you go?	Yes. Trinity Church is an active Episcopal church with a full schedule of worship services Sun-F. The church is open to visitors every day 8-6, and the churchyard is open from 8-sunset every day.	
Designations:	New York City Landmark (1966) National Historic Landmark (1976) National Register of Historic Places (1976)	

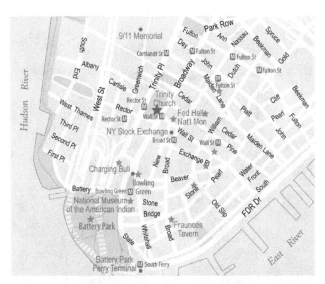

History/Items of Interest:

The charter for the parish was received on May 6, 1697 from the Royal Governor of New York. The first Trinity Church was built in 1698 as the first Anglican Church in Manhattan (the first rector was William Vesey). Trinity then built St. Paul's Chapel up Broadway in 1766 (to address Manhattan's exploding population).

The church was destroyed in the Great New York City Fire of 1776 (making St. Paul's the only remaining colonial-era church in Manhattan and the oldest public building in continuous use in the city). The New York State legislature ratified the church's charter in 1784. Services were held in St. Paul's until the second Trinity Church was constructed in 1790. After his inauguration in 1789, *George Washington* prayed in St. Paul's Chapel (members of the government, including *Alexander Hamilton* and John Jay, worshipped here while the capital was in New York). Hamilton's funeral procession on July 14, 1804 ended at Trinity Church, where he was eulogized by Gouverneur Morris and laid to rest.

The second church was torn down in 1839 (due to structural problems), and the third Trinity Church was built in 1846 – this is the current church. Trinity Church was the tallest building in New York until 1890 (when the New York World Building passed it). During the 9/11 attacks, the church acted as a refuge for people fleeing falling wreckage and debris.

Alexander Hamilton, *Eliza Hamilton*, *Philip Hamilton*, *Angelica Schuyler,* and *Hercules Mulligan* are all buried in the churchyard, but note that Angelica is buried on the other side of the church.

BAYARD'S MANSION

Location for: *The World Was Wide Enough – Act II*

Alexander Hamilton was taken here after his duel with Aaron Burr, and Angelica Schuyler and Eliza Hamilton "were both by his side as he died" here.

Who was *really* there?	Alexander Hamilton Eliza Hamilton Angelica Schuyler
Location:	80-82 Jane Street
Subway:	① ② ③ Ⓐ Ⓒ Ⓔ 14th Street Ⓛ 8th Ave.
Can you go?	Yes and no. The building pictured above is on the site of William Bayard's house, and there is a plaque on the wall of the building commemorating Hamilton's death.

History/Items of Interest:

William Bayard, Jr. was a prominent New York City banker and a close friend of *Alexander Hamilton* (he was a Bank of New York director). There is not much of note about the house itself other than as the site where Hamilton died.

After his duel with *Aaron Burr* the morning of July 11, 1804, Hamilton was rowed across the Hudson River to Bayard's dock and taken into his home. As word of the duel and Hamilton's mortal wound spread throughout the city, people congregated in front of Bayard's mansion. Bulletins providing updates on Hamilton's condition were circulated throughout the day.

Eliza Hamilton was summoned from the Grange to be by his side, and *Angelica Schuyler* joined her there. Hamilton was also attended there by doctors, several friends and clergy members. By all accounts, Hamilton was of clear mind and able to speak throughout the day.

The following day, all of Hamilton's children were brought into the room where he lay so that he could say goodbye to them. Hamilton's room was filled with friends and family throughout the day.

Hamilton died that day, July 12, 1804, in the early afternoon and more than a full day after the duel. A state funeral was held for him on July 14th, and after a procession through downtown New York City he was buried in the churchyard of Trinity Church.

Bit of trivia – some say that Bayard's mansion would have been located a block north of Jane Street, on present-day Horatio Street.

HAMILTON'S OTHER NEW YORK CITY RESIDENCES

26 Broadway, just opposite Broadway from Arturo Di Modica's *Charging Bull* statue

Location for: *Dear Theodosia – Act I*
Non-Stop – Act I
Schuyler Defeated – Act II
Hurricane – Act II
The Reynolds Pamphlet – Act II
Burn – Act II
Your Obedient Servant – Act II
Best of Wives and Best of Women – Act II

Each of these songs has Alexander Hamilton and/or Eliza Hamilton singing, and the context would indicate that at least a portion of the dialogue (or Hamilton's writing) would have taken place at his residence.

Who was *really* there?   Alexander Hamilton
Eliza Hamilton
Philip Hamilton
Angelica Schuyler

Location: 57-58 Wall Street
26 Broadway
54 Cedar Street

Subway: ① ® Rector Street; ② ③ ④ ⑤ Wall Street;
Ⓙ Ⓩ Broad Street

Can you go?   No – none of these buildings remain, and there are no commemorative plaques relating to Hamilton at these locations.

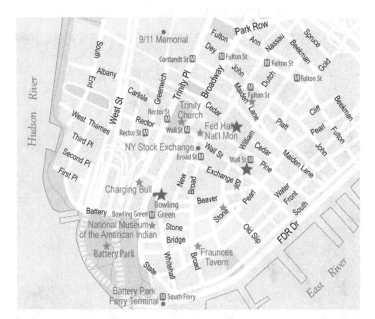

History/Items of Interest:

<u>57-58 Wall Street</u>
Alexander Hamilton, *Eliza Hamilton* and *Philip Hamilton* lived here after the American Revolution, until the nation's capital was moved to Philadelphia in December 1790. Hamilton lived here when he wrote *The Federalist Papers* in 1787-1788.

<u>26 Broadway</u>
Hamilton, Eliza and Philip lived here after Hamilton resigned from his role as Treasury Secretary in January 1795.

<u>54 Cedar Street</u>
Hamilton had a townhouse here. He wrote his final note to Eliza and spent the night here before his fateful duel with *Aaron Burr*.

Liberty Plaza (where 54 Cedar Street would have been)

HAMILTON'S NEW YORK CITY OFFICES

Stone Street (stone-paved pedestrian street in Lower Manhattan)

Location for: *Non-Stop – Act I*
Election of 1800 – Act II
Your Obedient Servant – Act II

Each of these songs has Alexander Hamilton singing, and the context would indicate that at least a portion of the dialogue (or Hamilton's writing) would have taken place at his office.

Who was *really* there?   Alexander Hamilton
Eliza Hamilton

Location: 36 Greenwich Street
69 Stone Street
12 Garden Street (now Exchange Place)

Subway: ① ® Rector Street; ② ③ ④ ⑤ Wall Street;
Ⓙ ❷ Broad Street

Can you go?   No – none of these buildings remain, and there are no commemorative plaques at these locations.

Designations: New York City Landmark (1996) – Stone Street is protected as a Historic District

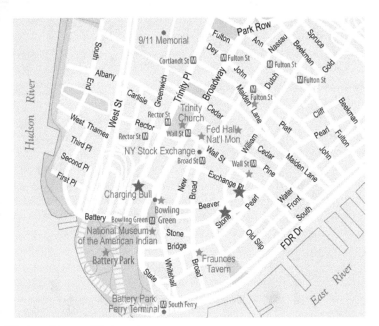

History/Items of Interest:

36 Greenwich Street

Alexander Hamilton worked out of this office during his time as general and second-in-command under *George Washington*, who was appointed to command a new American army in 1798. Washington delegated Hamilton the responsibility and authority to form the new army, which Hamilton did with his typical attention to minutiae with respect to all aspects of the army.

He continued to practice law out of this office, including during the Levi Weeks trial in 1800, when he acted as co-counsel for the defendant along with *Aaron Burr*.

69 Stone Street

Hamilton had his law office here at the time of *Philip Hamilton*'s duel with George Eacker, as well as when he was working on having the Grange built and the associated property landscaped. Stone Street is now a pedestrian street with lots of bars and restaurants and would be a good place for a rest during your visit and to "raise a glass to freedom" in Hamilton's memory.

12 Garden Street

This was Hamilton's final law office, and he spent his last days getting his affairs and those of his law clients in order before his duel with Aaron Burr. He was in this office when he received Burr's initial letter demanding an explanation for statements attributed to Hamilton.

CHAPTER TWO

OTHER NEW YORK CITY LOCATIONS
OF NOTE TO *HAMILTON*

...you're here with us in New York City

The following New York City locations are not particularly important with respect to the content of *Hamilton: An American Musical*, but they are of note with respect to the show itself.

MORRIS–JUMEL MANSION

Location for: *Right Hand Man – Act I*

George Washington and his men have "gotta run to Harlem quick" following the Battle of Long Island. He "runs" to Morris-Jumel Mansion, which serves as his temporary headquarters.

Who was *really* there?	Aaron Burr Alexander Hamilton Thomas Jefferson George Washington
Location:	Roger Morris Park, 65 Jumel Terrace
Subway:	① 157th Street © 163rd Street ® © 155th Street
Can you go?	Yes. The building is operated as a museum and is open from 10-4 T-F and from 10-5 Sat/Sun (though it is closed some holidays). There is an admission fee for the museum, and there are guided tours (for an additional fee; morrisjumel.org or 212-923-8008 for reservations).
Designations:	New York City Landmark (1967/1975) National Historic Landmark (1961) National Register of Historic Places (1966)

History/Items of Interest:

The Morris-Jumel Mansion was built in 1765 by Colonel Roger Morris, and the estate was named "Mount Morris." Mount Morris was one of the highest points in Manhattan, with clear views of New Jersey, Connecticut, and all of New York harbor (which was to make it a strategic military location).

The Morrises had to leave their home during the American Revolution due to their Tory sympathies. Following the Battle of Long Island, *George Washington* made the house his headquarters from September 14 to October 21 of 1776. From this strategic position, he planned his army's first successful victory – The Battle of Harlem Heights (though the Continental Army was soon forced to leave Manhattan by the British). After Washington's army abandoned Manhattan Island, the house served as headquarters to the British. After the war, the property was confiscated by the U.S. government and then purchased by Stephen Jumel in 1810, who lived there with his wife, Eliza Bowen.

After Jumel died in 1832, Eliza married *Aaron Burr*, though the marriage was short-lived and Eliza filed for divorce in 1833. Eliza lived in the house until her death in 1865. In 1904, the city of New York purchased the house and turned it into a museum.

Today, the Morris-Jumel Mansion is the oldest remaining house in Manhattan and is a museum highlighting over 200 years of New York history, art, and culture.

Lin-Manuel Miranda was granted a writing space at the mansion, and he wrote a portion of *Hamilton* during his time there.

RICHARD RODGERS THEATRE

Location for: *Greatest Show on Earth*

Who was there? Everyone, (almost) every night

Location: 226 West 46th Street

Subway: ❶ 50th Street

                 ❶ ❷ ❸ ❼ Times Square – 42nd Street

                 Ⓝ Ⓠ Ⓡ Ⓢ Times Square – 42nd Street

                 Ⓐ Ⓒ Ⓔ 42nd Street – Port Authority

Can you go?   Good luck getting tickets, and don't forget about the online lottery (see details at hamiltonbroadway.com). In August 2016, they stopped doing the Ham4Ham live performances at the theatre prior to the Wednesday matinee shows (but follow @HamiltonMusical on Twitter for updates; they may decide to do them again – it was a great way to see cast members perform live).

History/Items of Interest:

The Richard Rodgers Theatre opened in 1924 as the 46th Street Theatre, and it was renamed in 1990 to honor the composer Richard Rodgers.

The most important part of history for the Richard Rodgers Theatre (at least for the readers of this book) is of course being the Broadway venue of *Hamilton: An American Musical*. The show opened at the theatre on August 6, 2015, after a hugely successful run at the Public Theater and has set the box office record for the Richard Rodgers Theatre. The theatre is also the site of the #Ham4Ham live show, which takes place outside the theatre during the Wednesday matinee live lottery and features cast members and special guests (which are often performers from other Broadway shows).

The Richard Rodgers Theatre already had a history of successful shows before *Hamilton* arrived. The theatre currently holds the distinction of having housed the greatest number (eleven) of Tony Award-winning Best Plays and Best Musicals (including *Hamilton*, after its 2016 Tony Best Musical win), more than any other theatre on Broadway. Also on this list is **Lin-Manuel Miranda**'s first Broadway show, *In The Heights*, which won the 2008 Tony Award for Best Musical, as well as Tony winners *Guys and Dolls* (1951) and *Damn Yankees* (1956), and the theatre was also the venue for the *Chicago* revival when it won the 1997 Tony Award for Best Revival of a Musical.

THE PUBLIC THEATER

Location for: *New York City debut of* Hamilton

Who was there? Everyone who could manage to get tickets

Location: 425 Lafayette Street

Subway: ④ ⑥ Astor Place

        Ⓠ Ⓡ Ⓦ 8th Street Station

Can you go?   Yes, and you should! The Public Theater continues the work of its founder Joe Papp and presents a wide breadth of programming in its six venues, and regularly debuts award-winning shows destined for Broadway. See publictheater.org for the current slate of shows.

Designations: New York City Landmark

History/Items of Interest:

The Public Theater was founded in 1954 as the Shakespeare Workshop, and was opened as The Public Theater in 1967. The Public is housed in the Astor Library Building, which was built between 1853 and 1881.

Like the Richard Rodgers Theatre, the most important part of history for The Public Theater for *Hamilton* fans is being the venue for the New York City opening of *Hamilton: An American Musical*. The show had a sold-out run in the Newman Theater at The Public from January 20, 2015 until May 3, 2015, before transferring to Broadway and the Richard Rodgers.

Also like the Richard Rodgers Theatre, The Public had a history of successful shows before *Hamilton*. Including Hamilton, more than 50 productions have moved from The Public Theater to Broadway, with the most commercially successful being *Hair* (1967), *A Chorus Line* (1975) and, of course, *Hamilton* (2015). The Public has six different venues - Joe's Pub, Anspacher Theater, LuEsther Hall, Martinson Theater, Newman Theater and Shiva Theater - and don't miss the chance to have a drink or dinner at The Library before a show. The Public also runs Shakespeare in the Park, a New York City tradition providing free performances at The Delacorte Theater in Central Park for more than 60 years.

Location for: *The Tony Awards*

Who was there? The Original Broadway Cast of *Hamilton*, at the 2016 Tonys

Location: 2124 Broadway

Subway: ❶ ❷ ❸ 72nd Street/Broadway

Can you go? Yes. The Beacon Theatre is an operating venue and regularly hosts concerts and comedy and other shows. See msg.com/beacon-theatre for a calendar of show. The Box Office is open M-Sat from 11 to 7, and closed Sun.

Designations: National Register of Historic Places (1982)

History/Items of Interest:

The Beacon Theatre opened in 1929 as a movie theater and vaudeville venue. In addition to being a regular venue for live music and other performances, to date it has hosted the Tony Awards in 2011, 2012 and 2016.

Most relevant to this book, The Beacon Theatre was the venue for the 70th Annual Tony Awards held on June 12, 2016. *Hamilton* received 16 nominations (a record), winning 11 in total, including Best Musical, Leading Actor in a Musical (Leslie Odom Jr.), Featured Actor in a Musical (Daveed Diggs), Featured Actress in a Musical (Renee Elise Goldsberry), Best Book of a Musical, Best Original Score, Best Costume Design of a Musical, Best Lighting Design of a Musical, Best Direction of a Musical, Best Choreography and Best Orchestration.

The Schuyler Sisters and *History Has Its Eyes on You/Yorktown* from Hamilton were among the performances during the show, and the decision was made to perform *Yorktown* without the muskets used during the Broadway show, in recognition of the 2016 Orlando nightclub shooting, which occurred earlier that same morning. It was during his acceptance speech that **Lin-Manuel Miranda** included his "Love is love is love is love is love is love is love is love" phrase that became a mantra against the senseless violence and intolerance that has become more and more prevalent in our society.

CHAPTER THREE

OTHER ALEXANDER HAMILTON RELATED THINGS TO SEE AND DO IN NEW YORK CITY

...we just happen to be in the greatest city in the world

There are a lot of other places in the city that someone interested in Alexander Hamilton's life may be interested in visiting, even though they don't have any real connection with *Hamilton: An American Musical*. Some of them are listed in the following pages.

MUSEUM OF AMERICAN FINANCE

Location: 48 Wall Street

Subway: **1** **R** Rector Street
              2 **3** **4** **5** Wall Street
              J **Z** Broad Street

Visitor Info: The museum is open 10-4 T-Sat, and there is an admission fee (kids under 6 are free) – see moaf.org for more info. **UPDATE: As of October 2019, the museum is closed and seeking a different permanent location - check moaf.org for current information before going.**

Why go there?   There is a room dedicated to Alexander Hamilton (Hamilton's Legacy) containing various Hamilton artifacts (e.g., his debt assumption report and a reproduction set of the pistols from his duel with Aaron Burr). And don't skip the museum shop, where you can pick up an Alexander Hamilton tie or bobblehead.

NEW-YORK HISTORICAL SOCIETY

Location: 170 Central Park West (at 77th Street)

Subway: **1** 79th Street; **2** **3** 72nd Street;
              B **C** 81st St – Museum of Natural History

Visitor Info: The museum is open 10-6 T-Th and Sat, 10-8 F and 11-5 Sun, and there is an admission fee for the museum (kids under 5 are free) – see nyhistory.org for more info.

Why go there?   The museum has several Hamilton-related artifacts in its regular collection, and they host Hamilton-themed exhibits from time to time. The museum commemorated the bicentennial of Hamilton's death in 2004/5 with the exhibit "Alexander Hamilton: The Man Who Made Modern America," and the museum's 2016 "Summer of Hamilton" celebrated all things Hamilton in recognition of the success of *Hamilton: An American Musical* and Ron Chernow's biography (in addition to exhibiting artifacts from outside the museum's collection, the museum held special exhibitions and events).

COS CLOTHING STORE

Location: 129 Spring Street

Subway:  6 Spring Street

N R Prince Street

C E Spring Street

Visitor Info: The store is open 10-8 M-Sat and 11-7 Sun.

Why go there? This one's a bit out there. In the basement of the store is the 200+-year old "haunted" well involved in the Levi Weeks murder case (where Alexander Hamilton and Aaron Burr served as defense counsels for Weeks). The woman Weeks was accused of murdering was found in this well, and there have been reports of strange happenings around the well over the years.

MUSEUM OF THE CITY OF NEW YORK

Location: 1220 Fifth Avenue (at 103rd Street)

Subway: 4 5 6 103rd Street

Visitor Info: The museum is open 10-6 every day, and there is an admission fee for the museum (ages 19 and under are free) – see mcny.org for more info.

Why go there? The museum has a permanent collection of portraits of many Revolution-era people, including Alexander Hamilton and George Washington, and the museum had a special portrait exhibit in 2016 that featured these portraits (call the museum at 212-534-1672 for info on current exhibits). Don't miss the statue of Hamilton outside the museum (near the corner of 104th Street), and don't forget to look at the museum shop's Hamilton-related prints.

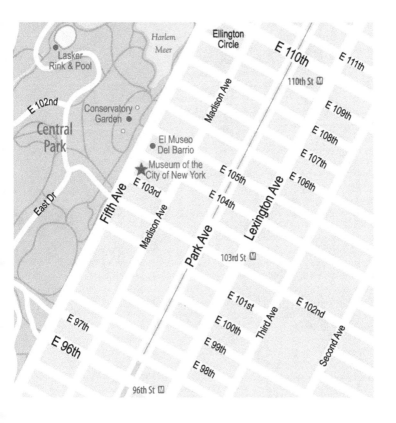

CHAPTER FOUR

HAMILTON LOCATIONS
IN NEW JERSEY

Everything is legal in New Jersey

Many of the events depicted in the show occurred in New Jersey (mainly during the American Revolution, as George Washington and his troops camped in New Jersey for several periods during the war). While you may be tempted to stick with the New York City locations, the more adventurous of you may be willing to venture over to New Jersey to see some of the locations that are of particular importance to the life of Alexander Hamilton and the content of *Hamilton: An American Musical*.

WEEHAWKEN, NEW JERSEY

Setting for: *Blow Us All Away – Act II*
Stay Alive (Reprise) – Act II
The World Was Wide Enough – Act II

The fateful duel between Philip Hamilton and George Eacker happens in Blow Us All Away. *Philip sings that he "was aiming for the sky" in recounting the duel to Alexander Hamilton in* Stay Alive (Reprise). *The duel between Aaron Burr and Alexander Hamilton, where Hamilton was mortally wounded, also occurs here in* The World Was Wide Enough.

Who was *really* there?   Aaron Burr
Alexander Hamilton
Philip Hamilton

Location: South of Hamilton Park (at JFK Boulevard East and Hamilton Avenue)

Subway/Bus: ❶ ❷ ❸ ❼ Times Square – 42nd Street
Ⓝ Ⓠ Ⓡ Ⓢ Times Square – 42nd Street
Ⓐ Ⓒ Ⓔ 42nd Street – Port Authority

From Port Authority, take NJ Transit bus 165, 166 or 168 to Hamilton Park, Boulevard East at Bonn Place (20 minutes).

Can you go?   Yes. You can visit Hamilton Park for an unobstructed view of the Manhattan skyline. You can also see the Hamilton Monument and plaques commemorating the Hamilton-Burr duel along Hamilton Avenue (just south of Hamilton Park).

History/Items of Interest:

Philip Hamilton

The duel between *Philip Hamilton* and George I. Eacker occurred on November 23, 1801 at what is now Weehawken, NJ. Eacker, a Republican lawyer, gave a speech at a July 4th celebration that year, during which he "disparaged [Philip's] father's legacy in front of a crowd." Philip saw the speech and the references to Hamilton. Philip encountered Eacker several months later, at the Park Theater in lower Manhattan, and he and a friend confronted Eacker about the speech, which led to duel challenges from both men, and Eacker accepted both.

The duel between Philip's friend and Eacker occurred first, ending with four missed shots. Attempts to negotiate a truce for Philip failed, leading to the duel in Weehawken the next day. Hamilton advised Philip to reserve his fire, and Eacker mortally wounded Philip with his first shot. Philip was taken to the home of John and Angelica Church, where he died the following day (with both parents at his side).

Alexander Hamilton

The much more famous duel between *Alexander Hamilton* and *Aaron Burr* occurred on July 11, 1804 on the same site in Weehawken. Contrasting Philip's duel, which occurred three days after he confronted Eacker, Alexander's duel with Burr was long in the making. The two men shared a lifetime of disagreements and contention, primarily concerning politics, and politics was at the heart of the matter that finally pushed Burr to challenge Hamilton.

Hamilton had opposed Burr's campaign to become governor of New York in 1804 (which Burr lost). In June 1804, Burr learned of injurious statements Hamilton had allegedly made about Burr, which given his recent political defeat were the last straw. On June 18th, Burr and William Van Ness met at Richmond Hill, and Van Ness delivered a letter to Hamilton at his Garden Street office that day demanding an explanation of Hamilton's statements. The two men exchanged several letters to no avail, and Van Ness delivered a duel request to Nathaniel Pendleton (for Hamilton) on June 27th. The duel was set for July 11th so Hamilton could attend to his law practice and put his affairs in order. He spent the night before the duel at his Cedar Street townhouse.

As he had advised Philip, Hamilton decided to "throw away his shot" and reserve his fire. And as it had for Philip, this decision proved fatal, as Burr's first shot mortally wounded Hamilton (like Philip, Hamilton was shot above his right hip). He was taken to the home of William Bayard, where he died the following day, July 12th, and where "Angelica and Eliza were both at his side when he died." He was buried in the churchyard at Trinity Church on July 14th, after a funeral procession through lower Manhattan.

MORRISTOWN, NEW JERSEY

Setting for: *Right Hand Man – Act I*
A Winter's Ball – Act I
Helpless – Act I
Satisfied – Act I

George Washington invited Alexander Hamilton to be his aide-de-camp in Morristown in 1777, as sung in Right Hand Man. *Washington used Ford Mansion as his headquarters during much of the winter of 1779/1780; Hamilton also lived here and attended nearby dances, such as the one sung about in* A Winter's Ball, Helpless *and* Satisfied. *Eliza Schuyler lived at the Schuyler-Hamilton House during that winter, and much of Hamilton's courtship of her as sung in* Helpless *happened here.*

Who was *really* there?	Alexander Hamilton
Eliza Hamilton
Philip Schuyler
George Washington
Location:	Ford Mansion – 230 Morris Avenue
Schuyler-Hamilton House – 5 Olyphant Pl.
Subway/Train:	❶ ❷ ❸ Ⓐ Ⓒ Ⓔ 34th St. – Penn Station

From Penn Station, take New Jersey Transit (Morris & Essex Line) to Morristown. |
| **Can you go?** | Yes. You can visit Ford Mansion (which is part of Morristown National Historical Park) W-Sun from 9:30-5, and there are tours of the mansion (first-come, first served). The Schuyler-Hamilton House is open Sundays from 2-4 (tours can be arranged) – call (973) 539-7502 for more info. |

History/Items of Interest:

Ford Mansion

The winter of 1779/1780 was worse than the famous winter in Valley Forge (it remains the only time in recorded history that the waters around New York City froze over). *George Washington* used the mansion of Judy and Jacob Ford in Morristown as his headquarters that year. *Alexander Hamilton* also stayed in the mansion. However, the winter may have contributed to the social scene at the mansion, as Washington hosted dinners and receptions there that attracted guests, including young women, as an escape from the harsh weather – Hamilton was a regular attendee at these events. During this winter Washington and his officers attended nearby balls, which may have been frequented by *Eliza Schuyler*.

Schuyler-Hamilton House

During the winter of 1779/1780, Eliza's aunt, together with her husband, Dr. John Cochran (surgeon general of the Continental Army), stayed at the home of Dr. Jabez Campfield. Eliza arrived in Morristown in February 1780 and stayed with the Cochrans for the winter. Having already met Eliza in Albany, Hamilton began to socialize with Eliza soon thereafter. Hamilton used his vast intellect, charm and writing abilities to court Eliza, and she was helpless to resist – they decided to get married little more than a month after Eliza's arrival. Eliza's father, *Philip Schuyler* arrived in Morristown in April and likely visited the house (though he and his wife resided elsewhere while in Morristown). The house was purchased by the Morristown chapter of the New Jersey Daughters of the American Revolution in 1923 and renamed in honor of Eliza Schuyler and Alexander Hamilton.

The Green

The Morristown Green now has the feel of a neighborhood park, but at one time it was a hub of military activity during Washington's first winter in Morristown with his Continental Army in 1777. It was here at Jacob Arnold's Tavern, on January 20, 1777, that Washington invited Hamilton to join his staff as an aide-de-camp (advancing Hamilton to the rank of lieutenant colonel upon his official appointment on March 1, 1777) – a plaque marks the original location of the tavern. Fans of the show may also want to visit the park to see the group of life-size statues of Washington, Hamilton and the *Marquis de Lafayette* (depicting Lafayette informing Washington and Hamilton on May 10, 1780 that the French would be coming to support the Americans in their fight against the British). The Green is located approximately one mile due west of the Ford Mansion (you can reach it by going along Lafayette Avenue).

BATTLE OF MONMOUTH – NEW JERSEY

Setting for: *Stay Alive – Act I*

George Washington and his Continental Army snatched "a stalemate from the jaws of defeat" here.

Who was *really* there?
Aaron Burr
Alexander Hamilton
Marquis de Lafayette
John Laurens
Charles Lee
George Washington

Location:
Border of Freehold Township/Manalapan Township

Can you go?
Yes. Monmouth Battlefield State Park preserves the historical battlefield where this battle was fought. The park is open daily from 8-6 during Fall/Spring, from 8-4:30 during Winter and from 8-8 during Summer (the Visitor Center is open 9-4 daily). There is an annual reenactment of the 1778 Battle of Monmouth at the park in late June (check out njparksandforests.org for info).

Designations:
New Jersey Register of Historic Places (1971)
National Historic Landmark District (1961)
National Register of Historic Places (1966)

History/Items of Interest:

The opportunity for this battle arose when the British army under General Henry Clinton decided in June 1778 to evacuate Philadelphia and retreat to New York (which required that they cross New Jersey). *George Washington* recognized that the retreating British army could be vulnerable to attack during their slow move across New Jersey. Despite reservations from his war council, Washington decided to attack if the opportunity presented itself. General *Charles Lee* initially refused to serve as Washington's second in command and only relented after Washington assigned the position to the *Marquis de Lafayette*.

Lee was ordered to attack the British, who were camped near Monmouth Court House in Freehold, NJ, the morning of June 28, 1778 (*Alexander Hamilton* drafted Washington's order). Washington would bring up the rear with the main force of the army.

While Lee did in fact attack the rear guard of the British army (under General Cornwallis), Washington arrived to find Lee's troops in full retreat. Washington took command of Lee's men and rallied them to hold off the British until the main force was able to arrive (Washington had ridden ahead after receiving word of Lee's retreat).

The heat of the day added to the stress of battle, as Washington's white charger died from the heat (forcing him to take up a new horse). Hamilton, *John Laurens* and *Aaron Burr* all had their horses shot from under them, and Burr was stricken with sunstroke that ended his combat duty for the rest of the war.

The battle is considered to have essentially been a draw (as the British were able to continue their retreat), but it served to truly cement Washington as a war hero and skilled commander, and it established Hamilton as courageous and unflappable in battle. Lee was arrested for disobeying orders and eventually subjected to a court martial (which led to his suspension from the army for one year). Lee spoke out regularly against Washington (and, to a lesser extent, Hamilton), ultimately leading to Laurens challenging Lee to a dual that occurred outside of Philadelphia on December 23, 1778, as sung in *Ten Duel Commandments* (with Hamilton serving as Laurens' second).

Of note is that the legend of "Molly Pitcher" is associated with this battle. One version has Mary Ludwig Hays, the wife of a local American artilleryman, bringing water for the crews and cannons and taking her husband's place in the battle after he died. Look for markings on the battlefield of "Molly Pitcher's Spring."

The Snyder Academy of Elizabethtown

Setting for: *Aaron Burr, Sir – Act I*

Even though the lead-in to Aaron Burr, Sir *says "1776 – New York City," both Alexander Hamilton and Aaron Burr had similar contacts in Elizabethtown (now split into Elizabeth and Union) during 1773 and may have had their initial meeting there.*

Who was *really* there?   Aaron Burr
Alexander Hamilton
Marquis de Lafayette
George Washington

Location: Snyder Academy – 42 Broad St., Elizabeth
Boxwood Hall – 1073 East Jersey St., Elizabeth
Liberty Hall – 1003 Morris Avenue, Union

Subway/Train: ❶ ❷ ❸ Ⓐ Ⓒ Ⓔ 34th St. – Penn Station

From Penn Station, take New Jersey Transit (New Jersey Coast or Northeast Corridor Lines) to Elizabeth.

Can you go?   Yes. Snyder Academy has a small museum room and offers campus tours – both typically require appointments (call (908) 353-2131 to make arrangements). Boxwood Hall is open M-F from 9-noon and 1-5 (call (908) 282-7617 to confirm hours). Liberty Hall Museum is open M-Sat from 10-4 from April-December (there is an admission fee – call (908) 527-0400 for more info).

History/Items of Interest:

The Snyder Academy of Elizabethtown

Through letters of introduction provided by Rev. Hugh Knox, shortly after arriving in New York *Alexander Hamilton* found his way to the Elizabethtown Academy, where he completed his college preparatory studies. He was following in *Aaron Burr*'s footsteps, who attended the school several years earlier, and his first meeting with Burr may have occurred in Elizabethtown. The school's headmaster, Francis Barber, would later fight in the Battle of Yorktown, serving under Hamilton.

Boxwood Hall

Through another of Knox's letters, Hamilton was introduced to Elias Boudinot and became a frequent visitor to Boxwood Hall, Boudinot's home, during his time in Elizabethtown. *George Washington* had lunch here in April 1789, before heading to New York for his inauguration. During his return visit to the States in 1824, the *Marquis de Lafayette* spent the night at Boxwood Hall.

Liberty Hall

Yet another Knox letter introduced Hamilton to William Livingston, and Hamilton lived with Livingston and his family during at least part of his time in Elizabethtown (though likely in temporary housing during the construction of Liberty Hall). In addition to introducing Hamilton to society (and possibly influencing Hamilton's political views), Livingston and his family played many roles in Hamilton's life.

Livingston's son Brockholst was co-counsel with Hamilton and Burr during the Levi Weeks trial. Livingston's brother-in-law, Lord Stirling, was the first to approach Hamilton to be his military aide, in 1776 (Hamilton declined), and he would later command his vastly outnumbered troops in the Battle of Brooklyn, fighting long enough to allow Washington to ferry most of his forces across the East River. Lord Stirling briefly commanded Hamilton's artillery company (before Hamilton became Washington's aide-de-camp) and even presided over Charles Lee's court martial (at which Hamilton was a witness against Lee; Burr, by contrast, submitted a letter defending Lee). John Jay, co-author of *The Federalist Papers*, was Livingston's son-in-law. Finally, Livingston's daughter Kitty was an early recipient of Hamilton's amorous attentions, and she may have played a key role in bringing Hamilton and Eliza Schuyler together, as she was a friend of both.

Liberty Hall Museum is 1-1/2 miles northwest of the other two sites. You can reach it by going along Morris Ave., and there are two buses (26/52) that get you most of the way there (and back). Visit the Alexander Hamilton room, where he was often a guest.

PATERSON, NEW JERSEY

Mentioned in: *Take A Break – Act II*
Say No to This - Act II

While Take A Break *follows* Cabinet Battle #1 (*about Alexander Hamilton's debt plan*), Hamilton was actually working on his Report on Manufactures *during 1791 (when Eliza Hamilton takes the kids to "all go stay with [her] father" in Albany) - this report led to the establishment of Paterson as the nation's first industrial city. Hamilton is "someone under stress" in* Say No to This *due to his work on the report and his efforts to establish Paterson.*

Who was *really* there?	Alexander Hamilton Marquis de Lafayette George Washington
Location:	Paterson Great Falls National Historical Park - 72 McBride Avenue, Paterson
Subway/Bus:	❶ ❷ ❸ ❼ Times Square – 42nd Street Ⓝ Ⓠ Ⓡ Ⓢ Times Square – 42nd Street Ⓐ Ⓒ Ⓔ 42nd Street – Port Authority
	From Port Authority, take NJ Transit bus 161 or 190 to Market Street (45 minutes).
Can you go?	Yes. Paterson Great Falls National Historical Park is operated by the National Park Service and has ranger-led tours and a Welcome Center. Call 862-257-3709, or visit hamiltonpartnership.org or nps.gov/pagr for more info.

History/Items of Interest:

Alexander Hamilton, *George Washington* and the *Marquis de Lafayette* visited the Great Falls of the Passaic River on July 10, 1778, shortly after the Battle of Monmouth. While there they enjoyed a brief break from war and a picnic lunch of ham, tongue, "excellent" biscuits and grog. Washington and Hamilton would return to Great Falls during the Revolutionary War in 1780, and Lafayette visited Great Falls during his visit to the States in 1824.

Like so many other locations with a connection to Hamilton, the Great Falls would reappear in a later episode of his life. Hamilton submitted his *Report on Manufactures* to Congress in December 1791, in which he advocated the development of American industry as necessary to reduce reliance on foreign powers and to gain economic independence for the country. The report was nearly two years in the making, during which time Hamilton was laying the groundwork for its success. Hamilton began to acquire British manufacturing knowledge in 1790-91, and he was instrumental in the creation in late 1791 of the Society for the Establishment of Useful Manufactures (S.U.M.). The S.U.M. was the first corporation in New Jersey and was chartered to promote manufacturing by providing land, mill buildings and water power.

In Hamiltonian fashion, Hamilton was involved in almost all aspects of the project. He supported the S.U.M.'s initial stock offering to secure funding, he initiated the search for the site for the town and he selected Pierre L'Enfant (fresh off his role as planner for the new federal capital that would later become Washington, D.C.) as town planner. While Hamilton may have remembered the area from his wartime visits, it was the river's power and the 77-foot tall, 300-foot wide Great Falls that led him to select it as the site for the world's first city planned for industry. The charter (written mostly by Hamilton) for the new town of Paterson around the Great Falls was granted on November 22, 1791 – the town was named for New Jersey Governor William Paterson.

Initially losing money (which Hamilton, encouraging "Perseverance," had predicted), the S.U.M. became successful and remained so for 150 years, and Paterson manufactured the first Colt revolvers, silk, locomotives, submarines, aircraft engines and many goods Hamilton listed in his *Report on Manufactures*. Hamilton's report also noted that manufacturing would promote immigration, which he favored as a means to bring a "diversity of talents" to the country and because, as Hamilton would say (and prove), "Immigrants. We get the job done."

In recognition of the importance of Paterson as the realization of Hamilton's vision for an industrial America, legislation creating the Paterson Great Falls National Historical Park was signed by President Obama in 2009, and the park was established in 2011.

CHAPTER FIVE

HAMILTON LOCATIONS
IN PHILADELPHIA

Congress is fighting over where to put the capital...

Philadelphia became the temporary site of the nation's capital following the passing of the Residence Bill of 1790, and the government was relocated from New York City to Philadelphia in late 1790. While this is not made clear during *Hamilton* (Philadelphia is not mentioned once in the show), a lot of the events depicted in the show took place in Philadelphia, so there's a lot to see there (in addition to the role the city played during the American Revolution and the founding of our country generally).

INDEPENDENCE HALL

Setting for: *Non-Stop – Act I*
Cabinet Battle #1 – Act II

Independence Hall is where Hamilton heads after he is "chosen for the Constitutional Convention," sung about in Non-Stop. *When Jefferson sings that he wrote about "life, liberty and the pursuit of happiness" in* Cabinet Battle #1, *he wrote about them at Independence Hall.*

Who was *really* there?	John Adams Alexander Hamilton Thomas Jefferson John Laurens James Madison George Washington
Location:	520 Chestnut Street
Directions:	SEPTA: 5th St. Independence Hall-MFL PATCO: 8th & Market Street Station
Can you go?	Yes. Independence Hall is part of Independence National Historical Park, run by the National Park Service. Open daily 9-5 (9-7 in summer) except on government holidays. Free guided tours last approximately 1/2 hour. In busy months, free timed tour tickets for Independence Hall must be acquired at the Independence Visitor Center.
Designations:	US National Historic Landmark (1966) UNESCO World Heritage Site (1979)

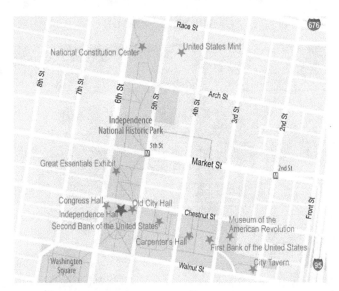

History/Items of Interest:

Independence Hall (IH) was built between 1732 and 1751 and served as the Pennsylvania State House until 1799.

In May 1775, the thirteen colonies sent representatives to IH to form the Second Continental Congress. In June, *John Adams* nominated fellow delegate *George Washington* as commander-in-chief of the Continental Army. Adams and *Thomas Jefferson* were on the committee to draft the Declaration of Independence, which was approved at IH on July 4, 1776.

Congress met at IH intermittently throughout the war. On one occasion, *Alexander Hamilton* wrote to Congress warning them to evacuate the city. Congress left just ahead of the British. During the British occupation, the building served as barracks and a hospital for wounded American prisoners. The British abandoned Philadelphia in 1778, and the Continental Congress returned to IH. In December of 1778, Washington and his military aides, including *John Laurens* and Hamilton, spent six weeks in Philadelphia.

The Constitutional Convention, to revise the Articles of Confederation, was held in IH in 1787. Hamilton, *James Madison*, and Washington were among the delegates, with Washington presiding as Convention President. The Convention ended on September 17, 1787 with the delegates signing the Constitution.

In 1816, the building was transferred from the state to the city of Philadelphia, which still owns the building. IH was restored in 1948 to its 18th century appearance and established as part of Independence National Historical Park.

CARPENTERS' HALL

Setting for: *Farmer Refuted – Act I*
Cabinet Battle #1 – Act I

In the song Farmer Refuted, *Alexander Hamilton is engaged in a debate with Samuel Seabury, which in real life took place through a series of written pamphlets. In these essays, Hamilton supported the actions of the First Continental Congress, which did not speak for Seabury and which had recently convened at Carpenters' Hall. Later in* Cabinet Battle #1, *Hamilton discussed his proposal to create a national bank, which rented space in Carpenters' Hall in the 1790s.*

Who was *really* there?	John Adams Alexander Hamilton George Washington
Location:	320 Chestnut Street
Directions:	SEPTA: 5th St. Independence Hall-MFL PATCO: 8th & Market Street Station
Can you go?	Yes. Carpenters' Hall is open 10-4, Tues-Sun (closed Tues in Jan/Feb) with free admission.
Designations:	National Register of Historic Places (1970) National Historic Landmark (1970)

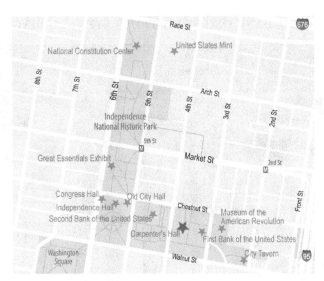

History/Items of Interest:

Carpenters' Hall, built between 1770 and 1774 for what is now the country's oldest extant craft guild, served many important roles in its history. Just after completion, it was the location for the First Continental Congress, a gathering of representatives from twelve of the thirteen colonies to discuss resistance the British Intolerable Acts. Attendees included *John Adams* and *George Washington*.

After the First Continental Congress, other important political meetings were held at Carpenters' Hall, and institutions rented out space in the building. Some of these early institutions included the American Philosophical Society, the Bank of North America, and the Library Company, the nation's first successful lending library founded by Benjamin Franklin and others.

As Treasury Secretary, *Alexander Hamilton* proposed the creation of a national bank. Despite fierce opposition from James Madison and Thomas Jefferson, the act to create the Bank of the United States was signed into law in 1791. The First Bank building, however, was not completed until 1797. During much of the interim, the bank rented space in Carpenters' Hall. Hamilton's office was on the same block, so his frequent interactions with the First Bank's leaders likely brought him to Carpenters' Hall.

After the Bank of the United States left Carpenters' Hall, it continued to serve as a rental space (including for the Second Bank of the United States) until 1857 when the Carpenters' Company restored the building and opened it to the public as a historic monument - the first of its kind. Today the Carpenters' Company still owns the building and maintains the first floor as a museum.

70

FIRST BANK OF THE UNITED STATES BUILDING

Mentioned in: *Cabinet Battle #1 – Act II*

In Cabinet Battle #1, *Hamilton's proposal for a national bank was on the table for debate.*

Who was *really* there?   Unknown

Location: 116 South 3rd Street

Directions: SEPTA: 5th St. Independence Hall-MFL PATCO: 8th & Market Street Station

Can you go?   Yes and no. You can view the outside of the building, but the interior is currently closed to the public (as of 2019). The First Bank Restoration Project is working to restore and open the building as a museum on Alexander Hamilton's legacy and early US financial history.

Designations: National Register of Historic Places (1966)
National Historic Landmark (1987)

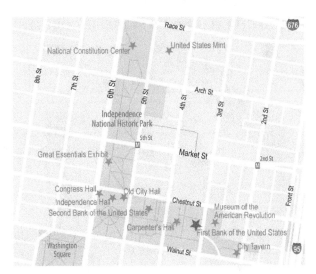

History/Items of Interest:

As part of his economic program, *Alexander Hamilton* submitted to Congress on December 13, 1790 his Second Report on Public Credit, which included his recommendation to establish a national bank. He believed a national bank was necessary to manage public funds and regulate financial institutions, and that it would stimulate the economy, boost national credit, and create a national currency.

The legislation faced opposition from leaders such as James Madison, and George Washington sought the opinions of his cabinet on whether it should be signed into law. Secretary of State Thomas Jefferson and Attorney General Edmund Randolph argued that the Constitution did not permit the charter of a bank. Washington took these arguments to Hamilton, who produced the 13,000 word "Opinion on the Constitutionality of an Act to Establish a Bank," providing the constitutional rationale for the creation of a national bank. His wife Eliza stayed up all night the last night copying out Hamilton's writing, and the report was submitted the next day to Washington. After reading Hamilton's report, Washington signed the bill into law on February 25, 1791.

The First Bank initially rented out space, principally at Carpenters' Hall, to run its operations. Construction of the First Bank Building began in 1795 and was completed in 1797, and the bank operated there until 1811, when Congress did not renew its charter. Most of the bank's assets were sold to Stephen Gerard, who ran the Gerard Bank out of the same building. The Gerard Bank remained there until 1929. The National Park Service purchased the deteriorating building in 1955 to become a part of Independence National Historical Park and restored it during the country's bicentennial.

OLD CITY HALL (OLD SUPREME COURT)

Plaque at Old City Hall

Mentioned in: *Non-Stop – Act I*

The song Non-Stop *mentions Alexander Hamilton's career as a lawyer. In 1796, Hamilton argued a case in the U.S. Supreme Court, then convening at the Old City Hall.*

Who was *really* there?   Alexander Hamilton

Location: Corner of Chestnut Street and Independence Mall East (5th Street)

Directions: SEPTA: 5th St. Independence Hall-MFL PATCO: 8th & Market Street Station

Can you go?   Yes. The Old City Hall is part of Independence National Historical Park. Free admission. In order to tour Old City Hall, pass through the security clearance to the Independence Hall complex at the corner of Chestnut and 5th Street. Open daily 9-5 except on government holidays.

Designation: US Historic District Contributing Property (Independence National Historic Park)

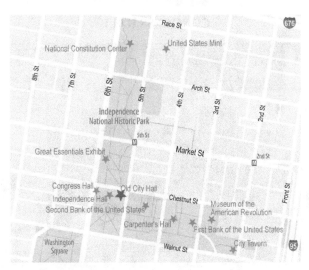

History/Items of Interest:

Philadelphia's Old City Hall was constructed next to the Pennsylvania State House, better known as Independence Hall, between 1790-91. When Philadelphia served as the nation's capital in the 1790s, the second floor of City Hall was used by the federal court system, including the US Supreme Court, which handed down the nation's first Supreme Court decisions from the building.

One of the first major cases brought to the Supreme Court was Hylton v. United States in 1796. The issue at hand was whether a law passed by Congress in 1794 levying a tax on carriages was a direct tax, and therefore not permitted by the Constitution. Though *Alexander Hamilton* had retired as Treasury Secretary, he was asked to return from New York to argue on behalf of the federal government. One justice remarked that Hamilton's 3-hour speech was "attended by the most crowded audience I ever saw…though he was in very ill health, he spoke with astonishing ability…and was listened to with the profoundest attention." The court agreed with Hamilton's argument that the tax was not a direct tax and upheld the law. This case was the first test of the constitutionality of a law, seven years before Marbury v. Madison. Hamilton's arguments inside Old City Hall contributed to the precedent of judicial review, which became a pillar of the US judicial system.

When the national capital moved to D.C. in 1800, the courts moved with them. The building continued to function as City Hall until 1854. Today, Old City Hall is still owned by the city, but leased as part of Independence National Historical Park. The second floor is restored to represent how the chambers would have looked when the Supreme Court met there between 1791-1800.

CONGRESS HALL

House Chamber at Congress Hall

Location for: *I Know Him – Act I*
                    The Adams Administration – Act II

The songs I Know Him *and* The Adams Administration *discuss John Adams succeeding George Washington as President. Adams was inaugurated at Congress Hall.*

Who was *really* there?

John Adams
Aaron Burr
Alexander Hamilton
Thomas Jefferson
James Madison
George Washington

Location: Intersection of Chestnut Street and 6th Street

Directions: SEPTA: 5th St. Independence Hall-MFL PATCO: 8th & Market Street Station

Can you go?   Yes. Congress Hall is part of Independence National Historical Park. Free admission. In order to tour Congress Hall, pass through the security clearance to the Independence Hall complex at the corner of Chestnut and 5th Street. Open daily 9-5 except on government holidays.

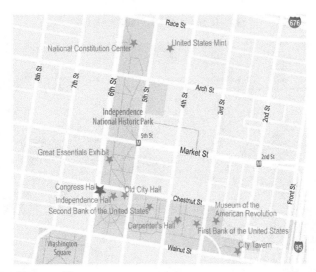

History/Items of Interest:

Congress Hall, which was originally constructed in 1789 as the Philadelphia County Courthouse, hosted both the US House of Representatives and the US Senate while the national capital was located in Philadelphia from 1790 to 1800. Those who served in Congress Hall during this time include *James Madison* in the House and *Aaron Burr* in the Senate (after winning Philip Schuyler's seat in *Schuyler Defeated*). Both *John Adams* and *Thomas Jefferson* served as President of the Senate in Congress Hall during their terms as Vice-President.

Congress often asked Treasury Secretary *Alexander Hamilton* to submit reports recommending new fiscal and economic programs to be considered for legislation. Hamilton would also meet with congressional committees in Congress Hall to discuss some of his proposals. Many of Hamilton's seminal reports, including the Report on the Establishment of a Mint, Report on a National Bank, Report on Manufacturing, and the Report on Furthering Public Credit were submitted and debated in Congress Hall. Some of the government's earliest institutions, such as the First Bank of the United States and the US Mint, were established as a result.

Other significant events occurred in Congress Hall during this time, including the passage of the Bill of Rights, the ratification of the Jay Treaty, and the acceptance of three new states to the union. *George Washington* had his second inauguration in Congress Hall in 1793 and four years later he attended as Adams was sworn in as President. The interior of the House of Representatives chamber has been restored to its 1797 appearance to pay homage to the historical significance of this peaceful transfer of power to Adams.

OFFICE OF THE TREASURY

Plaque marking site of Treasury Office

Setting for: *Cabinet Battle #2 – Act II*
Washington on Your Side – Act II

During the timeframe of Cabinet Battle #2 *and* Washington on Your Side, *Alexander Hamilton was working as Secretary of the Treasury at this office site.*

Who was *really* there? Alexander Hamilton

Location: 100 South 3rd Street

Directions: SEPTA: 5th St. Independence Hall-MFL PATCO: 8th & Market Street Station

Can you go? No and yes. The building no longer stands, but a brick outline of the foundations still stands marking the spot, and a plaque along the iron fence on South 3rd Street facing the foundations describes the site.

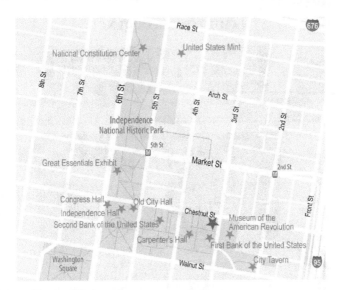

History/Items of Interest:

When the US capital moved from New York City to Philadelphia in late 1790 - thanks to the dinner deal as depicted in *The Room Where It Happened* - the Treasury Secretary moved along with the rest of the government. While still in New York, *Alexander Hamilton* had friends search for office space in Philadelphia. He settled on a large two-story brick house at the corner of 3rd Street and Chestnut Street. The building, owned by a merchant named Daniel Coxe, had previously been rented as a home to the President of Congress and would be converted to office space for Hamilton and his staff.

From this office, Hamilton wrote some of his seminal reports, including "Report on a National Bank," "Report on the Establishment of a Mint," "Report on Manufacturing," and "Report on the Further Support of Public Credit." In addition, Hamilton worked from this site to make many of his proposed institutions a reality, including the Bank of the United States and the Revenue Cutters (the early US Coast Guard). Hamilton also continued his work establishing the US Customs Service, the Lighthouse Establishment, and the country's taxation system. He also provided advice to George Washington's administration in matters such as the strategy and defense of the Jay Treaty and the Proclamation of Neutrality, as well as the response to the Whiskey Rebellion.

Hamilton worked out of this office from October 1790 until January 31, 1795, when he retired from his position as Treasury Secretary to return to New York City and resume his law practice. His successor, Oliver Wolcott, Jr., worked in the building until the national capital was moved from Philadelphia to D.C. in 1800.

HAMILTON'S RESIDENCE

Plaque marking site of Hamilton's Residence

Setting for and   *Take a Break – Act II*
Mentioned in: *Say No to This – Act II*
                       We Know – Act II
                       The Reynolds Pamphlet – Act II

Eliza Hamilton took the children to upstate New York in the summer of 1791 while Alexander Hamilton stayed at their rented home in Philadelphia to work, as detailed in the song Take a Break. *It was during this summer that Hamilton's affair with Maria Reynolds began, with their meetings often occurring at the Hamiltons' house in* Say No to This.

Who was *really* Alexander Hamilton
there?   Eliza Hamilton
                       Philip Hamilton
                       Maria Reynolds
                       Angelica Schuyler

Location: Southeast corner of Walnut Street and South 3rd Avenue

Directions: SEPTA: 5th St. Independence Hall-MFL PATCO: 8th & Market Street Station

Can you go?   No and yes. Though the home no longer stands, a building at approximately the home's location has a plaque commemorating Hamilton's former residence.

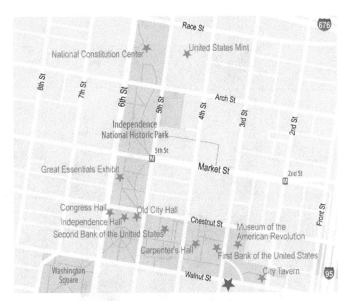

History/Items of Interest:

When the national capital moved from New York City to Philadelphia in the fall of 1790, Secretary of Treasury *Alexander Hamilton* and his family had to relocate along with the federal government. While searching for a house in the new capital city, Hamilton's biggest desire was to have his home near his Treasury offices (see the page on Treasury Office). Other items on his wish list included "a cool situation and exposure...at least six rooms, good dining and drawing rooms...elbow room in a yard. As to rent the lower the better." Hamilton was able to find a home that fit enough of his requirements near the intersection of Walnut and South 3rd Street, just a block away from his Treasury offices.

The Hamilton family moved into the house in October 1790. Hamilton and *Eliza Hamilton* lived in this rented home with their children *Philip Hamilton*, Angelica, Alexander Jr, James Alexander, and their adopted daughter Fanny Antil. The Hamiltons also hosted politicians, business leaders, and friends. In the summer of 1791, another visitor came to the house - *Maria Reynolds.* She sought an audience with Hamilton to explain that she had been abandoned by her husband and needed some monetary assistance. When Hamilton later brought her some money, they began an affair. Maria often would come over to the Hamilton house while Eliza and the children were away visiting her family in upstate New York that July and August.

The Hamilton family lived in the house until mid-August of 1791, when they moved to a new home in Market Street that they rented from merchant Philip Stein.

CITY TAVERN

Setting for: *Right-Hand Man – Act I*
    Non-Stop – Act I

Alexander Hamilton stayed at City Tavern several times in his capacity George Washington's aide-de-camp, the position he took during the song Right-Hand Man. *After the war, as mentioned in the song* Non-Stop, *Hamilton became a delegate to the Constitutional Convention in Philadelphia and spent time at City Tavern after sessions to meet and strategize with fellow delegates.*

Who was *really* there?	John Adams Alexander Hamilton Thomas Jefferson John Laurens Marquis de Lafayette James Madison George Washington
Location:	138 South 2nd Street
Directions:	SEPTA: 5th St. Independence Hall-MFL PATCO: 8th & Market Street Station
Can you go?	Yes. Today visitors can stop at the reconstructed City Tavern to grab an 18th-century meal or 'Founding Fathers' brews served by period-dressed waiters. Open daily for lunch and dinner.

History/Items of Interest:

City Tavern was built through a subscription of Philadelphians desiring a respectable public gathering place. Opened in 1773, *John Adams* deigned it "the most genteel tavern in America." It quickly became a center of political life and served as a meeting place and lodgings for government officials. Delegates of the 1774 First Continental Congress, including *George Washington* and Adams, dined here after sessions to discuss policy, a practice that would continue with later bodies of Congress and politicians, including *Thomas Jefferson* and *James Madison*.

In July 1777, City Tavern hosted the country's first July 4th celebration. A month later, Washington and his staff, including *Alexander Hamilton*, set up headquarters there. The *Marquis de Lafayette* first met Washington and Hamilton there, which led to Washington inviting Lafayette to join his staff as aide-de-camp. Washington later wrote to *John Laurens* from there inviting him to serve as aide-de-camp. This was the beginning of the close friendship between the three aides.

Hamilton would stay at City Tavern on other occasions during the war, including when Washington sent him to requisition supplies from Philadelphians in September 1777. After the war, Hamilton would have spent time at City Tavern when he was a delegate to the Constitutional Convention (1787), Secretary of the Treasury (1790-95), and Major-General during the Quasi War (1798).

Around 1800, City Tavern became known as the Merchants Coffee House. The building was damaged by fire in 1834 and demolished in 1854. For the 1976 bicentennial, the National Park Service completed a historically-accurate reconstruction of the building, which is today a restaurant serving authentic period food.

SITE OF LEE-LAURENS DUEL

Present-day intersection near site of duel

Setting for: *Ten Duel Commandments – Act I*
                    Meet Me Inside – Act I

In Ten Duel Commandments, *Charles Lee and John Laurens face off in a duel - in real life it took place just outside Philadelphia. The confrontation with George Washington sung about in* Meet Me Inside *following the duel would have happened here.*

Who was *really* there?	Alexander Hamilton John Laurens Charles Lee
Location:	Near the intersection of present-day East Venango and Richmond Streets
Directions:	SEPTA: Allegheny Station-MFL
Can you go?	No. The duel took place in some woods near the four-mile stone marker of what was then called Point-no-Point Road (today at the intersection of Richmond Street and East Venango Street). The stone is no longer there.

History/Items of Interest:

Following the Battle of Monmouth in June 1778, *Charles Lee* was tried in a court martial for his conduct. He was found guilty of disobeying orders during battle. Angry at being removed from command as a result, he started to speak ill of George Washington. Washington's aide-de-camp *John Laurens* felt Lee's attacks went beyond criticizing Washington as a military leader - that Lee spoke of him "in the grossest and most opprobrious terms of personal abuse." Because of his respect for Washington, Laurens felt he should defend Washington's personal honor and hold Lee accountable for his slanders. Laurens asked fellow aide *Alexander Hamilton* to serve as his second. Lee's former aide Evan Edwards (not Aaron Burr, as depicted in the musical) served as Lee's second. The "affair of honor" was not resolved through mediation, and the four men met for a duel while they were all in Philadelphia.

The "interview" was arranged to take place in the woods four miles outside Philadelphia on the afternoon of December 23, 1778. After the first exchange of pistol fire, Lee was shot in the side. After examining his wound, he decided he wanted a second round of fire. While Laurens agreed, Hamilton and Edwards eventually convinced them both to end the duel and declare honor satisfied. Afterwards, the two aides wrote a detailed account of the duel, including a conversation after the exchange of pistol fire in which Lee swore he never spoke poorly of Washington as a man, but only as a military figure.

A portion of that account (regarding the exchange of fire and the decision to end the affair): "General Lee then said the wound was inconsiderable, less than he had imagined at the first stroke of the Ball, and proposed to fire a second time. This was warmly opposed both by Col Hamilton and Major Edwards, who declared it to be their opinion, that the affair should terminate as it then stood. But General Lee repeated his desire, that there should be a second discharge and Col Laurens agreed to the proposal. Col Hamilton observed, that unless the General was influenced by motives of personal enmity, he did not think the affair ought to be pursued any further; but as General Lee seemed to persist in desiring it, he was too tender of his friend's honor to persist in opposing it...Col Hamilton and Major Edwards withdrew and conversing awhile on the subject, still concurred fully in opinion that for the most cogent reasons, the affair should terminate as it was then circumstanced. This decision was communicated to the parties and agreed to by them, upon which they immediately returned to Town; General Lee slightly wounded in the right side."

CHAPTER SIX

ALEXANDER HAMILTON RELATED
THINGS TO SEE AND DO IN PHILADELPHIA

I will try to get away...

Just like New York, there are a lot of other places in Philadelphia that someone interested in Alexander Hamilton's life may be interested in visiting, even though they don't have any connection with *Hamilton: An American Musical*. Some of them are listed in the following pages.

MUSEUM OF THE AMERICAN REVOLUTION

Location: 101 South 3rd Street

Directions: SEPTA: 5th St. Independence Hall-MFL PATCO: 8th & Market Street Station

Visitor Info: The museum is open 9:30-5 daily, and there is an admission fee for the museum (children 5 and under are free). See amrevmuseum.org for more info.

Why go there?   This is the first museum dedicated to telling the story of the Revolutionary War in its entirety. Exhibits cover the origins of the war, its many theaters, and the aftermath of the country's founding. Special artifacts are on display that Alexander Hamilton himself would have used and seen, including George Washington's war tent, headquarters flag, and camp cups. Hamilton's role in the war is mentioned in several places in the museum.

NATIONAL CONSTITUTION CENTER

Location: 525 Arch Street

Directions: SEPTA: 5th St. Independence Hall-MFL PATCO: 8th & Market Street Station

Visitor Info: The museum is open daily; M-Sat 9:30-5, Sun 12-5. There is an admission fee (free for active military and children 5 and under). See constitutioncenter.org for more info.

Why go there? This museum is the first and only public institution dedicated to educating the public about the US Constitution. As a signer and one of the principal forces for the Constitution's ratification and implementation, Alexander Hamilton is mentioned throughout the principal exhibit space and has been featured in temporary exhibits at the museum as well. Don't miss a visit to Statuary Hall to hang out with a life-size statue of Hamilton and the other signers of the Constitution.

SECOND BANK BUILDING

Location: 420 Chestnut Street

Directions: SEPTA: 5th St. Independence Hall-MFL PATCO: 8th & Market Street Station

Visitor Info: The building is open 11-5 daily in the summer; if you're visiting other times of the year, check online at nps.gov to see the days it is open. Admission is free.

Why go there? The building is home to the Second Bank Portrait Gallery, which has more than 85 portraits on display. The "People of Independence" exhibit depicts many Revolutionary War leaders, including Alexander Hamilton, Thomas Jefferson, George Washington, James Madison, John Adams, the Marquis de Lafayette, and Philip Schuyler. Also see if you can find the miniature of John Laurens in a display case in one of the smaller rooms. Don't miss the exhibit that pays homage to Charles Willson Peale's collection from his Philadelphia Museum, which at one time was housed on the second floor of Independence Hall.

UNITED STATES MINT

Location: 151 Independence Mall East

Directions: SEPTA: 5th St. Independence Hall-MFL PATCO: 8th & Market Street Station

Visitor Info: The US Mint is open from 9-4:30, M-F. Admission is free. For visiting information and to download a self-guided tour brochure, visit usmint.gov. Note that the US Mint is a functioning government building, and you will have to pass through security and show a government-issued ID at the entrance.

Why go there? Alexander Hamilton's "Report on the Establishment of the Mint" led to passing of the Coinage Act of 1792, which created the US Mint. The US Mint's first location was in Philadelphia at the intersection of Seventh and Arch Streets. Today the Philadelphia branch of the US Mint allows visitors to view the coin-producing facilities and also has exhibits on the Mint's history, including a short video of Alexander Hamilton, Thomas Jefferson, and Benjamin Franklin discussing the creation of the US Mint.

GREAT ESSENTIALS EXHIBIT

Location: 520 Chestnut Street

Directions: SEPTA: 5th St. Independence Hall-MFL PATCO: 8th & Market Street Station

Visitor Info: Admission is free. In order to tour the Great Essentials Exhibit, pass through security to the Independence Hall complex at the corner of Chestnut and 5th Street. Open daily 9-5 except on government holidays.

Why go there?   Inside the Great Essentials exhibit, you will see rare original printings of the nation's three most important early documents: the Declaration of Independence, which asserted freedom from Great Britain; the Articles of Confederation, which was our country's first governing document; and the Constitution, which replaced the Articles of Confederation. Also in the room is the Syng Inkstand, which is believed to be the silver inkstand that was used by Thomas Jefferson, John Adams, and others to sign the Declaration of Independence in 1776, and by George Washington, James Madison, Alexander Hamilton, and others to sign the Constitution in 1787.

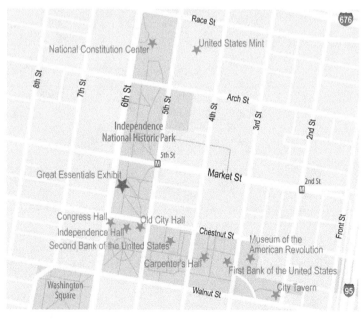

CHAPTER SEVEN

HAMILTON LOCATIONS
IN WASHINGTON, D.C.

The Virginians emerge with the nation's capital...

Philadelphia became the temporary site of the nation's capital as part of the Compromise of 1790, but the end result was the construction and ultimate relocation of the government to Washington, D.C. As with Philadelphia, it is not made clear in the show that some scenes depicted in the show would have taken place in Washington, D.C., as both the Adams and Jefferson administrations spent time in the city.

UNITED STATES CAPITOL

Setting for: *The Election of 1800 – Act II*

John Adams eagerly rushed to the new capital city in Washington DC, in the hopes that the new city would help his re-election prospects in 1800 (it did not).

Who was *really* there?	John Adams Thomas Jefferson James Madison George Washington
Location:	First Street NE and East Capitol Street
Metro:	Red Line: Union Station Orange/Blue Lines: Capitol South, Federal Center SW
Can you go?	Yes. The Capitol is open 8:30-4:30 M-Sat except on government holidays, and admission is free. Free guided tours are available. Reservations are recommended, and note that separate passes are required to visit the Senate or House Galleries (visitthecapitol.gov for more info).
Designations:	US National Historic Landmark (1960)

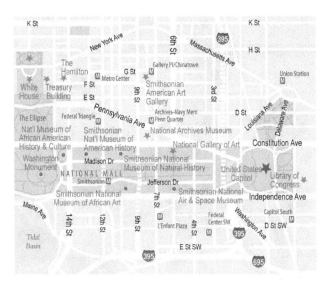

History/Items of Interest:

The site for the "Congress House" was selected by Pierre Charles L'Enfant, who created the plan for the nation's capital in DC. *Thomas Jefferson* changed the name to the "Capitol." The building's cornerstone was laid by *George Washington* in 1793.

Both houses of Congress convened in the incomplete Senate wing of the new Capitol for the first time on November 17, 1800. *John Adams* addressed Congress a few days later "on the prospect of a residence not to be changed." One New York senator stated that to make the new capital city perfect it needed only "houses, cellars, kitchens, well informed men, amiable women, and other little trifles of this kind." The House wing was not completed until 1807, and the building was finally completed in 1811.

Not too long after, the Capitol was one of the casualties of the War of 1812, when British troops set fire to the Capitol (as well as the White House) in 1814. Reconstruction began the following year and wasn't completed until 1826, although this included a redesign of the House and Senate chambers, as well as the Rotunda. The building has been expanded over the years, as more states were admitted, increasing the congresspeople to be accommodated. In addition to greatly increasing the building's footprint, the dome was replaced with a much larger dome in the mid-19th century.

The Library of Congress (1897) and the Supreme Court (1935) were eventually moved out of the Capitol to their own buildings. The most recent construction was the Capitol Visitor Center, which opened in 2008. Note that the Corinthian columns that formerly graced the Capitol can now be seen at the National Arboretum.

WHITE HOUSE

Setting for: *Who Lives, Who Dies, Who Tells Your Story*
– Act II

In the song Who Lives, Who Dies, Who Tells Your Story, *President Thomas Jefferson and President James Madison, both of whom lived in the White House during their presidencies, sing of their remembrances of Alexander Hamilton.*

Who was *really* there?	John Adams Thomas Jefferson James Madison
Location:	1600 Pennsylvania Avenue NW
Metro:	Blue/Orange/Red/Silver Lines: Metro Center
Can you go?	Yes. Public tour requests must be submitted through one's Member of Congress. These free self-guided tours are available from 7:30-11:30 a.m. T-Th, 7:30-1:30 F/Sat (excluding federal holidays). Foreign citizens can request tours through their embassy in D.C. Visit whitehouse.gov for more info.
Designations:	US National Historic Landmark (1960)

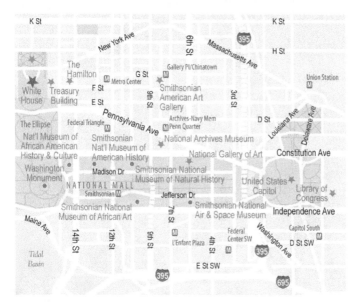

History/Items of Interest:

George Washington selected the site for the White House in 1791. The cornerstone was laid in 1792, and a design submitted by Irish-born architect James Hoban was chosen. After eight years of construction, President *John Adams* and his wife, Abigail, moved into the unfinished house in 1800. Every president since, including *Thomas Jefferson* and *James Madison*, has lived in the house.

During the War of 1812, the British set fire to the house in 1814. Hoban was appointed to rebuild the house, and President James Monroe moved into the building in 1817. During Monroe's administration, the South Portico was constructed in 1824, and Andrew Jackson oversaw the North Portico's addition in 1829.

At various times in history, the building has been known as the "President's Palace," the "President's House," and the "Executive Mansion." President Theodore Roosevelt officially gave the White House its current name in 1901. There are currently 132 rooms, 35 bathrooms, and 6 levels in the White House. There are also 412 doors, 147 windows, 28 fireplaces, 8 staircases, and 3 elevators.

Under the Obama administration, an evening of poetry, music and the spoken word was hosted at the White House on May 12, 2009, during which *Lin-Manuel Miranda*, accompanied by Alex Lacamoire, performed *Alexander Hamilton*, singing as Aaron Burr.

The original Broadway cast later performed at the White House on March 14, 2016 for the Obamas and a group of schoolchildren. They performed *Alexander Hamilton* and *My Shot*.

CHAPTER EIGHT

ALEXANDER HAMILTON RELATED
THINGS TO SEE AND DO IN WASHINGTON D.C.

Well I propose the Potomac…

Even though Alexander Hamilton never visited Washington, D.C., much of the nation's history was relocated to the city along with the government, and a lot of that history has a connection with Hamilton.

TREASURY BUILDING

Statue of Alexander Hamilton in front of Treasury Building

Location: 1500 Pennsylvania Avenue NW

Metro: Blue/Orange/Red/Silver Lines: Metro Center

Visitor Info: Free guided tours require advance reservations made through one's Senator or Representative and are only available to citizens and legal residents of the US. Tours last one hour and are given at 9, 9:45, 10:30 and 11:15 Sat mornings (excluding some holiday weekends). Note this is not the tour for seeing production of US currency notes/coins – book through US Mint. Visit home.treasury.gov/services/tours-and-library/tours-of-the-historic-treasury-building for more info. Tour highlights include the Andrew Johnson Suite and the Cash Room.

Designations: US National Historic Landmark (1971)

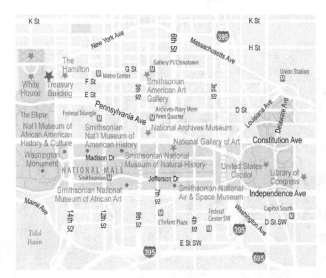

History/Items of Interest:

The original Treasury Building, a porticoed Gregorian-style building designed by an English architect, George Hadfield, was the only government building completed and ready for occupation when the federal government began to relocate from Philadelphia to Washington, D.C. in June 1800. The following year, a fire partially destroyed the building (which was to become a theme).

The building was eventually overrun by documents, and a fireproof vault extension was completed in 1806 on the building's west side. This proved fortunate, as the fireproof vault was the only part of the building that survived the attack by the British during the War of 1812, when they set fire to government buildings in 1814. The reconstruction of the Treasury Building, along with the other buildings burned during the war, was not completed until 1817.

An arsonist set fire to the building in 1833, and again the fireproof vault was key to the survival of the department's records. In July 1836, Congress authorized construction of a "fireproof building of such dimensions as may be required for the present and future accommodations" of the Treasury Department and construction was completed in 1842. The needs for the building were severely underestimated, with the South Wing (completed in 1861), West Wing (1864) and North Wing (1867) eventually being added.

The Treasury Building served as a temporary White House in 1865 when Andrew Johnson became president after the assassination of Abraham Lincoln. As a courtesy to Mary Todd Lincoln, Johnson delayed moving into the White House, allowing Mrs. Lincoln time to recover and plan her departure.

ANDERSON HOUSE

Location: 2118 Massachusetts Avenue, NW, Washington, DC 20008

Metro: Red Line: Dupont Circle

Visitor Info: The museum is open 10-4 T-Sat and 12-4 Sun and is closed most federal holidays (visit societyofthecincinnati.org for more info, including a schedule of events). Admission is free. Docent-led guided tours of the first and second floors of the house last approximately one hour and begin 15 minutes past each hour. The library is open 10-4 M-F. Anderson House also hosts exhibitions from time to time, and curator-led tours of such exhibitions may be available upon request.

Designations: US National Historic Landmark (1996)
US National Register of Historic Places (1971)
US Historic District Contributing Property

History/Items of Interest:

Anderson House was built in 1905 as the private residence of Larz Anderson, a Washington diplomat, with the modern conveniences at the time, including electricity, central heat and telephones. Anderson and his wife Isabel hosted dinners, luncheons, concerts, performances and diplomatic receptions at the house. Following Anderson's death in 1937, Isabel gave the house and its contents to the Society of the Cincinnati (Anderson had been a member).

The Society of the Cincinnati was founded in 1783 by Continental Army officers who served in the war. The Society's first meeting was chaired by *Alexander Hamilton*. The first President General was *George Washington*, who embodied the example of the Society's namesake, Lucius Quinctius Cincinnatus, a farmer who became dictator in time of crisis, but then willingly returned power to the Roman Senate to return to his farm. Washington served as President General from 1783 until his death in 1799, when Hamilton took over. Other early members included the Comte de Rochambeau, *Aaron Burr*, Nathanael Greene, Henry Knox, the *Marquis de Lafayette*, *Philip Schuyler*, and Baron von Steuben. Not all were in favor of the Society, and *Thomas Jefferson*, *John Adams* and Benjamin Franklin criticized the Society as an attempt to create an American nobility (as eligibility was tied to heredity).

Burr and Hamilton attended an 1804 4th of July dinner meeting of the Society at Fraunces Tavern less than a week before their duel. Hamilton was President General at the time. Accounts of the night paint Burr as silent and gloomy, whereas Hamilton was in high spirits and even sang for the group (likely "How Stands the Glass Around," an old military ballad).

NATIONAL PORTRAIT GALLERY

Location: 8th and F Streets NW

Metro: Yellow/Green/Red Lines: Gallery Place/Chinatown

Visitor Info: The gallery is open 11:30-7 daily (closed 12/25), with guided docent tours 12 and 2:30 M-F, 11:45, 1:30, 3:15 and 4:30 Sat/Sun and admission is free. See npg.si.edu/visit for more info.

Why go there? There is a John Trumbull portrait of Alexander Hamilton on display here. In addition, there are portraits of all of the presidents, so fans of the show can see George Washington, John Adams, Thomas Jefferson and James Madison portraits. There are also drawings of Aaron Burr and Marquis de Lafayette in the collection, though they may not be on display at any given time.

NATIONAL ARCHIVES BUILDING

Location: 701 Constitution Avenue, NW

Metro: Green/Yellow Lines: Archives-Navy Memorial-Penn Quarter

Visitor Info: The National Archives is open 10-5:30 daily (except Thanksgiving and Christmas) and admission is free (there is a $1 reservation fee for tours - reservations are not required but recommended, especially during the summer and holidays). Reserved docent-led guided tours are given at 9:45 M-F. See archives.gov/museum/visit/ for more info. No photos are permitted.

Why go there? The National Archives has on display the documents that were instrumental in the founding of the United States and which played a key role in the events of *Hamilton*. Alexander Hamilton played a key role in the Constitution, of which he was a signatory and which is on display. Don't miss "The Constitution," a mural in the Rotunda that includes Hamilton, George Washington and James Madison.

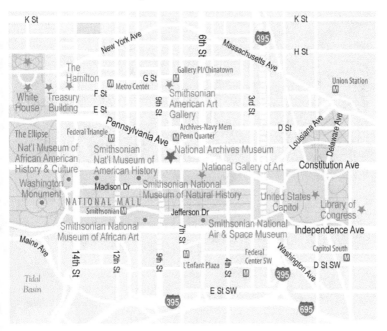

NATIONAL GALLERY OF ART

Location: 4th Street and Constitution Avenue NW (between 3rd/9th)

Metro: Green/Yellow Lines: Archives-Navy Memorial-Penn Quarter

Visitor Info: The gallery is open M-Sat 10-5 and Sun 11-6 (closed Christmas and New Year's Day). The Sculpture Garden is open seasonally (typically late August to mid-November, but see nga.gov for more info). Admission is free.

Why go there? There are a number of pieces on display from the Revolutionary War era, including a life-size portrait of George Washington on horseback on his way to the Battle of Yorktown. There is also a John Trumbull painting of Alexander Hamilton.

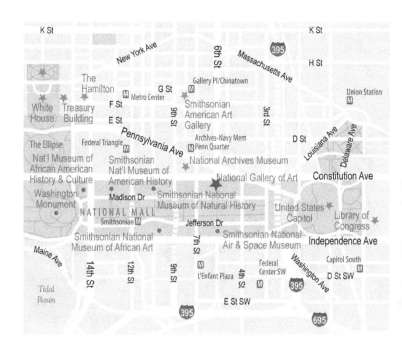

LIBRARY OF CONGRESS

Location: 10 First Street SE

Metro: Orange/Blue Lines: Capitol South, Federal Center SW

Visitor Info: The Library of Congress is open from 8:30-4:30, M-Sat (except Thanksgiving, Christmas and New Year's Day). There are numerous guided tours, including themed tours. Access to the Reading Rooms and Research Assistance varies. See loc.gov for more info on the above. The tours and most events take place in the Thomas Jefferson Building, but note that there are two other buildings.

Why go there? The Library itself has numerous talks, tours and events that should be of interest to anyone interested in Revolutionary history. But of particular interest to fans of *Hamilton* is the Alexander Hamilton Papers, a collection of approximately 12,000 items from throughout his life. The correspondents in these papers reads like the cast list from *Hamilton*.

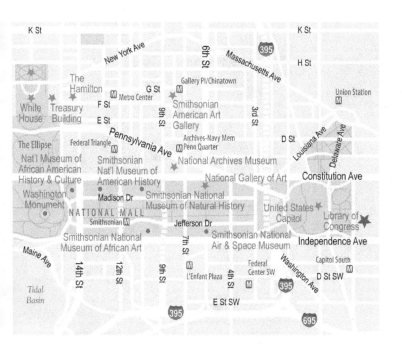

SMITHSONIAN INSTITUTION

Locations: Various

Metro: See map below.

Visitor Info: Admission is free to all Smithsonian museums and galleries. The hours vary depending on the location. See si.edu for more info.

Why go there? The Smithsonian Institution is the world's largest museum, education, and research complex, and the permanent collections on display include many items relevant to the events depicted in *Hamilton*. In addition, at any point in time there may be exhibits relevant to Alexander Hamilton, the founding of the United States or other events of interest to fans of the show or Hamilton (one example is the "Philanthropy and *Hamilton: An American Musical*" exhibit at the National Museum of American History). Don't overlook the Smithsonian - do a quick search at si.edu when planning your trip to see if an exhibit might interest you.

LAFAYETTE SQUARE

Location: Pennsylvania Avenue NW and 16th St NW

Metro: Blue/Orange/Red/Silver Lines: Metro Center
Blue/Orange/Silver Lines: McPherson Sq

Visitor Info: Lafayette Square is always open to public. See nps.gov/nr/travel/wash/dc30.htm for more info.

Why go there? Lafayette Square was named in honor of the Marquis de Lafayette. In addition to the statue of Lafayette in one of the four corners of the park, there are also statues of Comte de Rochambeau and Baron von Steuben, all Revolutionary War heroes. The park also provides a nice place to take a break and overlooks The White House (with the Washington Monument in the background). The park has been designated a US National Historic Landmark.

THE HAMILTON

Location: 600 14th Street, NW

Metro: Blue/Orange/Red/Silver Lines: Metro Center

Visitor Info: The Hamilton is open M-F 11-2; F-Sat 11-3; and Sun 10-2. See thehamiltondc.com for more info about events and for the restaurant menu.

Why go there?   For a fun meal or show. The Hamilton is a restaurant and event space with an Alexander Hamilton theme, but don't go expecting a lot of themed drinks or food - other than the logo and a drink name or two, there's not much of a connection. Still, it's a great restaurant (slightly upscale) in a central location, and they used to have logo pins (with Alexander Hamilton wearing sunglasses) - if you ask you may be able to score one.

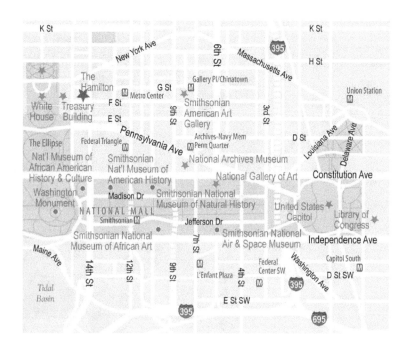

CHAPTER NINE

HAMILTON LOCATIONS
FURTHER AFIELD

The world was wide enough...

Many of the events depicted in the show occurred outside of New York City, New Jersey, Philadelphia and Washington, D.C. Many of these locations are of particular importance to the life of Alexander Hamilton and the content of *Hamilton: An American Musical*, so if you get a chance you may want to pay them a visit.

VALLEY FORGE, PENNSYLVANIA

Isaac Potts House at Valley Forge

Setting for: *Stay Alive – Act I*

When Alexander Hamilton writes to Congress that "we have resorted to eating our horses" in Stay Alive, *it's during a severe and bleak winter of the war, one of which was spent at Valley Forge.*

Who was *really* there?
Aaron Burr
Alexander Hamilton
John Laurens
Charles Lee
Marquis de Lafayette
George Washington

Location: 1400 N Outer Line Drive, King of Prussia, PA

Can you go?   Yes. Valley Forge is operated by the National Park Service and is open year-round with no admission fee. The parks grounds are open 7-sunset, and the Visitor Center is open 9-5 (9-6 during the summer; closed Thanksgiving, Christmas and New Years Day). See nps.gov/vafo for more info.

Designations: National Historical Park (1976)
National Historic Landmark District (1961)
National Register of Historic Places (1966)

History/Items of Interest:

The Continental Army under *George Washington* camped at Valley Forge during the 1777-1778 winter. Only a day's march from nearby Philadelphia (which was then occupied by British forces), Valley Forge was a naturally defensible area where the army could recoup until winter weather subsided to permit fighting to resume.

The Continental Army, some 12,000 strong, marched into Valley Forge the week before Christmas in 1777 (this number would grow to nearly 20,000 by the spring, as the army prepared to continue the campaign). While the army began to build what would essentially be the fourth largest city in the United States at the time, with 1,500 log huts and two miles of fortifications, *Alexander Hamilton* was still away on a critical mission on Washington's behalf to deliver orders to General Gates in order to arrange for immediate reinforcements to be sent from the northern troops to the main army camp near Philadelphia.

The Issac Potts house served as Washington's headquarters of during the encampment, and Washington's aides-de-camp, including Hamilton, *John Laurens* and the *Marquis de Lafayette*, also stayed and/or worked at the house. Martha Washington also stayed at the house during her time at Valley Forge that winter.

While conditions at Valley Forge were harsh - during the encampment, nearly 2,000 soldiers died, mainly from disease - it was over this winter that the army took major steps to becoming a more professional army. Washington was able to persuade Congress to reform the supply system and end the crippling shortages the army had grown accustomed to, by shrewdly getting a congressional committee to visit Valley Forge to gain a better understanding of the logistical difficulties Washington was forced to address in keeping the army intact and in condition to fight.

Another key accomplishment at Valley Forge resulted from Washington's appointment of the German-born Baron Friedrich Wilhelm von Steuben as acting inspector general of the main army. Von Steuben noted the army's lack of discipline and provided hands-on military training, established standards for camp layout and sanitation, and eventually wrote a complete military handbook. Hamilton and Laurens enthusiastically supported von Steuben's efforts and helped with interpretation and military language expertise. The army that emerged from Valley Forge was more disciplined and unified than the one that entered the encampment.

The army left the Valley Forge area devastated. When the army departed in June 1778, every tree for miles had been used for firewood or huts, along with miles of farmers' fences. The local livestock and stores had been commandeered, and they left behind roads, paths and refuse pits, not to mention about 2,000 huts.

YORKTOWN, VIRGINIA

Redoubt No. 10 at Yorktown

Location for: *Yorktown (The World Turned Upside Down)*
– Act II

Mentioned in: *Guns and Ships – Act II*
History Has Its Eyes on You – Act II
What Comes Next – Act II

Who was *really* there? Alexander Hamilton
Marquis de Lafayette
John Laurens
George Washington

Location: 1000 Colonial Parkway
Yorktown, VA 23690

Can you go? Yes. Yorktown Battlefield is part of the Colonial National Historical Park Virginia and preserves the historical battlefield where this battle was fought. Operated by the National Park Service, the park and the Visitor Center are open daily from 9-5 (except Thanksgiving, Christmas and New Years). See nps.gov/york for more info. There is a $10 fee for the Battlefield (under 15 free).

Designations: Virginia Landmarks Register
National Historic District
National Register of Historic Places (all as part of Colonial National Historical Park)

History/Items of Interest:

Yorktown was established in 1691 to regulate British trade and collect taxes for Virginia's colonial government, and by the early 18th century it had become a major port and economic center for Virginia. It boasted docks, shops and other businesses along the well-developed waterfront and had a population of about 2,000 by mid-century.

However, Yorktown's lasting place in our country's history is of course the central role it played as the location for the last major battle of the American Revolutionary War, as sung about in *Guns and Ships*, *History Has Its Eyes on You*, *Yorktown (The World Turned Upside Down)* and *What Comes Next*.

British general Lord Charles Cornwallis took his army to Yorktown in 1781 to establish a naval base there. While *Hamilton* only really describes the Siege of Yorktown, that siege was the culmination of months of moves and countermoves by the American, British and French forces. The ***Marquis de Lafayette*** moved his forces around the state, engaging and then retreating from the British forces, all while the French fleet was engaging with the British fleet in and around Chesapeake Bay to cut off Cornwallis' forces from reinforcement by sea.

George Washington arrived outside of Yorktown in mid-September (after a brief stop at Mount Vernon), by which time the French fleet had established command of the surrounding waters. The siege formally began on September 28, 1781, with the combined American and French armies marching out of Williamsburg to begin the assault on Cornwallis' positions. ***Alexander Hamilton*** was finally "in command where you belong" and in charge of a light infantry battalion during the siege. The siege was a couple of weeks old before Hamilton's main role came to pass – the attack on the British defenses at Redoubts No. 9 and 10 (the days before this was spent moving past the British outer defenses and moving the siege line within range of the Redoubts).

On October 14th, Hamilton led his men on a successful attack of Redoubt No. 10 with unloaded guns ("What!"), overtaking it in less than 10 minutes (Redoubt No. 9 was also successfully taken). With these successes, the American and French artillery were able to fire on Cornwallis' main forces, and the British surrendered on October 17th.

Yorktown was largely destroyed during the war, and a later fire and additional destruction during the Civil War kept it from ever regaining its pre-war prominence. Yorktown Battlefield is now part of the Colonial National Historical Park Virginia, run by the National Park Service.

WILLIAMSBURG, VIRGINIA

George Wythe House at Williamsburg

Setting for: *Yorktown (The World Turned Upside Down)*
– Act II

Alexander Hamilton was stationed in and around Williamsburg just before the Battle of Yorktown.

Who was *really* there?
Alexander Hamilton
Thomas Jefferson
Marquis de Lafayette
John Laurens
James Madison
George Washington

Location:
101 Visitor Center Drive
Williamsburg, VA 23185

Can you go?
Yes. Colonial Williamsburg is open year-round. Most historic trades and sites are open from 9-5 (the Visitor Center is open 8:45-5). There are also several evening programs available - these tend to be popular, and advance ticket purchases are recommended. There is an admission fee, but your ticket provides access to 40+ trades, sites and museums. See colonialwilliamsburg.com for more info.

Designations:
Virginia Landmarks Register (1969)
National Historic Landmark District (1960)
National Register of Historic Places (1966)

History/Items of Interest:

Williamsburg was founded in the early 17th century and served as the capital of Virginia from 1699 to 1780. As the capital of the most populous colony at the time leading up to the American Revolution, Williamsburg was of course central and influential to the American efforts.

Given its proximity to Yorktown, which was to be the decisive battle in the American Revolution, Williamsburg was a key location during the preparations for that final battle. *Alexander Hamilton* was briefly stationed in and around Williamsburg just before the Battle of Yorktown, along with much of the combined American and French forces that would participate in the battle. The two armies marched out of Williamsburg on September 28, 1781 to begin the siege of Yorktown.

The home of George Wythe, a leader of the patriotic movement in Virginia and a delegate to the Continental Congress, was located on Palace Green in central Williamsburg and served as the headquarters of *George Washington* just before the siege of Yorktown. It would later serve as headquarters for the Comte de Rochambeau following the victory at Yorktown and the British surrender.

The George Wythe House (or simply The Wythe House, as it is now known) also housed *Thomas Jefferson* when he was a delegate of the Virginia General Assembly in 1776, and was declared a National Historic Landmark in 1970. Jefferson also attended the College of William & Mary in Williamsburg and returned to serve as governor of Virginia in 1779 and 1780 (moving to Richmond when the capital of Virginia was moved there in 1780).

James Madison also attended the Fifth Virginia Convention in 1776, where the colony of Virginia became the first to vote for independence.

Colonial Williamsburg is now "the world's largest living history museum" and offers a glimpse into what colonial life in the 18th century would have been like. There are activities for all ages, and a number of different itineraries depending on your particular interest. They offer more than twenty different tours of their fifty or so different sites, trades and museums, so you may want to do some research before planning a trip, as there is much more to do there than can be done in a single day.

MOUNT VERNON, VIRGINIA

Mentioned in: *Right Hand Man – Act I*
Stay Alive – Act I

Following the Battle of Monmouth, Charles Lee spoke out against George Washington ("The pride of Mount Vernon" from Right Hand Man*) and sings in* Stay Alive *that Washington should "go back to planting tobacco at Mount Vernon."*

Who was *really* there?   Marquis de Lafayette
George Washington

Location: 3200 Mount Vernon Memorial Highway
Mount Vernon, Virginia 22121

Can you go?   Yes. Mount Vernon is open year-round. The site is generally open from 9-5 daily during the summer and from 9-4 daily during the winter, and there is an admission fee (under 5 are free). There are a number of different tours available, and for a different experience note that you can visit Mount Vernon by boat. Visit mountvernon.org for more info.

Designations: Virginia Landmarks Register (1969)
National Historic Landmark (1960)
National Register of Historic Places (1960)

History/Items of Interest:

The building to become the mansion at Mount Vernon began as a 1-1/2 story house built by *George Washington*'s father, Augustine Washington, in 1735. Washington's older (by 14 years) half-brother, Lawrence, inherited the property on their father's death in 1743 and renamed it from Little Hunting Creek to Mount Vernon to honor British Admiral Edward Vernon (who Lawrence served under). In order for George to take ownership of Mount Vernon, each of Lawrence, his wife, Anne, and all four of their children (including their offspring) had to pre-decease George. All of that had happened by 1761, when Anne died and Mount Vernon passed to George, who would own the property until his death in 1799.

By then Washington had leased Mount Vernon for several years (starting when Anne took ownership in 1754). Washington, whose meticulous attention to detail rivaled Alexander Hamilton's, expanded the building over time to a 21-room mansion with architectural features that reflected his growing status as a Virginia gentleman. The first major expansion was in 1758-59, when he added a story and refurbished the interior (mostly in his absence, as he led colonial soldiers during the French and Indian War).

The second major expansion began in 1775, just before the Revolutionary War (though it would not be completed until several years after the war) and gave Mount Vernon many of the features that make the mansion truly impressive. Wings on each end, the signature cupola (which was a departure from colonial styles of the time), several outbuildings, the collonades and the two-story piazza facing the Potomac River were all added as part of this expansion.

Washington did not get to spend much time in the completed mansion. The second expansion was largely overseen while he was away for the Revolutionary War (his only visits were brief visits before and after the siege of Yorktown in 1781), though he was able to oversee the completion of the work after the war. He was away again for the Constitutional Convention and while serving as our first president. He finally retired at Mount Vernon after his presidency in 1797, but died two years later. The *Marquis de Lafayette* visited Washington's grave at Mount Vernon during his 1824 return visit to the United States.

After Washington's death, Mount Vernon passed to his wife, Martha (who died three years later), and the property remained in the Washington family until acquired from Washington's great-great nephew by the Mount Vernon Ladies' Association (MVLA), now the nation's oldest historic-preservation organization, in 1858. The MVLA restored the property to its 1799 state (with some upgrades, like the installation of electricity, supervised by Thomas Edison, in 1916).

MONTICELLO, VIRGINIA

Setting for: *What'd I Miss – Act II*

When Thomas Jefferson sings "Virginia, my home sweet home, I wanna give you a kiss," *he's back home in Monticello from Paris.*

Mentioned in: *Cabinet Battle #1 – Act II*

Hamilton asks Jefferson if he wants to "stay mellow doing whatever the hell it is you do in Monticello."

Who was *really* there?   Thomas Jefferson
Marquis de Lafayette
James Madison

Location: 931 Thomas Jefferson Parkway
Charlottesville, VA 22902

Can you go?   Yes. Monticello is open year-round, generally 10-5 M-F, 8:30-6 Sat and 8:30-5 Sun (times change so see monticello.org for more info). You can only visit the house on a tour (and the tours offered change - they have offered a Hamilton themed tour in the past, so check what's available when you're there) - most have an admission fee (they have various discounts, and under 5 are free). There's a special ceremony on Jefferson's birthday (April 13th) every year.

Designations: UNESCO World Heritage Site (1987)
Virginia Landmarks Register (1969)
National Historic Landmark (1960)
National Register of Historic Places (1966)

History/Items of Interest:

Thomas Jefferson played a major role in the design of Monticello, and his influence touched every room in the building. Having inherited the land from his father, Jefferson had the mountaintop site cleared and leveled in 1768, and construction began the following year.

Jefferson was able to move into the South Pavilion (which is not part of the main house) in 1770. The north wing was the first part of the house itself to be completed and habitable, in 1772, and Jefferson's original design of the house had been completed by the time he left Virginia to serve as Minister of the United States to France.

It was during his time in Europe that Jefferson acquired many of the ideas, architectural and otherwise, that would guide his remodeling of his house. While in France, Jefferson became a regular companion of the ***Marquis de Lafayette***, who he helped draft a declaration until he said "I gotta be in Monticello" in *What'd I Miss*, and then left for home in 1789.

Jefferson's remodeling of Monticello had to wait until he finished his service as Secretary of State under ***George Washington***. And once he started, in 1794, Jefferson kept remodeling and rebuilding Monticello for the rest of his life. The primary expansion took place from 1796 through 1809, which saw the demolition of the upper story, the construction of the North Terrace, the South Terrace, the North Pavilion and the Dome, as well as the remodeling of the South Pavilion and the redecorating of much of the interior.

Jefferson often entertained friends and dignitaries at Monticello. ***James Madison*** and his wife, Dolley, visited Monticello so often that one of the guest bedrooms was known as Mr. Madison's Room, and their visits there would often last up to a month at a time. The Marquis de Lafayette visited Monticello in 1824 as part of his return trip to the United States, and he stayed for a couple of weeks (Madison was also visiting at the time, and James Monroe, president at the time, frequently visited Monticello during Lafayette's stay).

Monticello passed to Jefferson's daughter, Martha, upon his death, but she and her son were forced to sell the contents and then the plantation due to the massive debt that Jefferson died with, and it was ultimately purchased by Uriah Levy, a naval officer that admired Jefferson. The property was seized and sold by the Confederacy during the Civil War, though it was eventually returned to the Levy family after years of litigation. It was sold to the Thomas Jefferson Foundation in 1923, and it remains owned by the foundation today.

SCHUYLER MANSION

Setting for: *Satisfied – Act I*
The Story of Tonight (Reprise) – Act I

The wedding between Alexander Hamilton and Eliza Hamilton, as sung about in Satisfied, *took place at the Schuyler Mansion).*

Mentioned in: *Take A Break – Act II*

Eliza wanted them to "go stay with [her] father" in Take A Break. *Angelica Schuyler also could not convince Hamilton to join them upstate, despite coming all the way from England.*

Who was *really* there?
Alexander Hamilton
Eliza Hamilton
Philip Hamilton
Marquis de Lafayette
James Madison
Angelica Schuyler
Philip Schuyler
Peggy Schuyler
George Washington

Location: 32 Catherine Street, Albany NY

Can you go? Yes. At the time of this writing, the house is closed for general visits (re-opening May 2020). Guided tours are available by advance reservation, and special tours and school visits are available. For more info see parks.ny.gov/historic-sites/33/details.aspx. Most tours have an admission fee.

Designations: National Register of Historic Places (1967)
National Historic Landmark (1967)

History/Items of Interest:

Schuyler Mansion was constructed on eighty acres near Albany from 1761 to 1765 - the estate was known as the Pastures. The mansion was built as the residence of *Philip Schuyler*, who resided there from 1763 until his death in 1804. When they moved into the mansion, Schuyler and his wife, Catherine Van Rensselaer Schuyler, had three daughters - *Angelica Schuyler*, *Eliza Schuyler* and *Peggy Schuyler*.

Alexander Hamilton happened to visit the Schuyler Mansion, where he met Eliza, during a mission on behalf of George Washington in 1778. Hamilton would become reacquainted with Eliza during the winter of 1779/1780 when they were both in Morristown, New Jersey (see page 58 for more details). The wedding between Alexander Hamilton and Eliza Hamilton, which is part of the scene for *Satisfied*, took place at the mansion on December 14, 1780. Unlike the depiction in *Hamilton*, none of Hamilton's wartime friends that were characters in the show attended the wedding, as they were all too busy with their wartime duties.

Hamilton and Eliza's first child, *Philip Hamilton*, was born in the mansion in 1782, and they spent time visiting the mansion throughout their lives (though Hamilton was notably absent when he would not "run away with" Angelica and Eliza for the summer in *Take a Break*).

Several guests of note stayed at the mansion over the years, including *George Washington*, the *Marquis de Lafayette* and *James Madison*. The British General John Burgoyne was even temporarily housed there as a "prisoner guest" after his surrender at Saratoga.

After Philip Schuyler's death, the land of his estate was divided among his remaining children, but the mansion itself was sold. It changed hands over the years until it was eventually sold to New York State in 1911. The mansion was restored and opened to the public in 1917.

If you visit the mansion, don't forget to run your hand along the bannister during your visit - it's the original bannister, so there's a fair chance that you'll be touching something that Hamilton, Washington, Madison, Lafayette, Angelica and Eliza Schuyler (and Peggy) all touched.

NEVIS, ST. CROIX AND ST. EUSTATIUS

Setting for: *Alexander Hamilton – Act I*

Alexander Hamilton was born on the island of Nevis, though there is some disagreement as to the year he was born. In the spring of 1765, Hamilton and his family relocated to St. Croix, where the events sung about Hamilton's work in the trading charter in Alexander Hamilton *occurred. Thanks to research by Hamilton author Michael E. Newton, we now known that Hamilton also spent part of his childhood on the island of St. Eustatius (today known locally as Statia). He left St. Croix for New York City via a ship bound for Boston in the fall of 1772.*

Who was *really* there?   Alexander Hamilton

ENGLAND

Setting for: *You'll Be Back – Act II*
                    What Comes Next – Act II
                    I Know Him – Act II

King George III viewed the American Revolution from afar as sung in these three songs. The King had to deal with unrest in London when "the price of this war" became more than his people were willing to pay. He met John Adams, as he sings in I Know Him*, when Adams was appointed American Minister to London in 1785.*

Mentioned in: *Take A Break – Act II*

Angelica Schuyler arrives from London and tries to convince Hamilton to go to Albany with her and Eliza in Take A Break.

Who was *really* there?   Aaron Burr
                                Alexander Hamilton
                                King George III
                                Thomas Jefferson
                                James Madison
                                Angelica Schuyler
                                George Washington

CHARLESTON, SOUTH CAROLINA

No song from the cast recording, but there is a scene in the show depicting when ***Alexander Hamilton*** learns of the death of ***John Laurens***. Even though the British had surrendered at Yorktown in 1781, the British still held several cities in the South, including Charleston, South Carolina. In late August 1782, Laurens attacked a British foraging expedition outside of Charleston and was shot and killed in what is known as the Battle of the Combahee River, becoming one of the last casualties of the American Revolution.

CHAPTER TEN

OTHER ALEXANDER HAMILTON
RELATED THINGS

Can I show you what I'm proudest of?

In addition to the various locations related to *Hamilton* and Alexander Hamilton, there are other legacies and inspirations that originated from the incredible life led by Hamilton, one of the most influential of the founding fathers.

GRAHAM WINDHAM

Long before her star turn on Broadway, Eliza Hamilton helped establish "the first private orphanage in New York City," as sung about in *Who Lives, Who Dies, Who Tells Your Story?* Founded in New York City in 1806 by a group of dedicated forward-looking women, including Isabella Graham and Elizabeth Schuyler Hamilton, Graham Windham has been meeting the needs of New York City's poorest, most vulnerable children for more than two centuries!

Graham Windham serves over 4,500 kids and families each year — kids who like Eliza Hamilton's husband survived a rough start in life. Working with these kids, Graham Windham provides family counseling and treatment, after-school academic support, health services, and other services that help kids thrive into adulthood. You can help tell Eliza's story — join the Graham Windham community: http://elizasstory.org/

Visit graham-windham.org for more information about Graham Windham's approach and to find out ways to get involved or to make donations.

HAMILTON COLLEGE

Before the musical, there was Hamilton College. Located in Clinton, NY, more than 200 miles from the Richard Rodgers Theatre in New York City, Hamilton College was originally founded in 1793 with the support of Alexander Hamilton, who served as the institution's first trustee and lent his name to the college. He represented many of the qualities valued by his namesake college. The first Secretary of the Treasury and current Broadway sensation was an independent thinker, a persuasive writer and a powerful speaker whose effect on the new republic was lasting and profound. Today, the institution named for Alexander Hamilton is one of the most highly regarded liberal arts colleges in the United States.

Oh, and my daughter goes to Hamilton College (Class of 2021), so of course it's a great school.

HAMILTON: THE EXHIBITION

The success and genius of *Hamilton: An American Musical* has inspired a tremendous amount of interest in both Alexander Hamilton and in history related to the founding of our country. In order to address some of this interest, **Lin-Manuel Miranda**, Jeffrey Seller and David Korins, among many others, created Hamilton: The Exhibition, a "360-degree, immersive exhibit" inspired by Hamilton's life. Korins, the set designer for *Hamilton*, was the creative director and designer for The Exhibition. *Hamilton* received some criticism for some historical inaccuracies (which were necessary to make the show work and flow within the confines of a Broadway performance), so one focus of the creators of The Exhibition was to present even more history about Hamilton and the Revolution, but with a particular attention to the actual history (Yale history professor and Alexander Hamilton scholar Joanne Freeman served as an advisor for The Exhibition).

The Exhibition opened in Chicago in April 2019 and was meant to tour around the country - the massive exhibit was said to require in excess of 80 trucks to move. However, The Exhibition closed in August 2019 (slightly earlier than planned), and the plan to tour around the country may not come to fruition. The creators of The Exhibition are reportedly considering selling the exhibit to an operator, which could result in a fixed location. If you didn't get a chance to see The Exhibition during its run in Chicago, hopefully it will find a home somewhere and you will get a chance to see it - it really is very well done and a lot of fun, especially for fans of *Hamilton*.

THE HAMILCAST:
A HAMILTON PODCAST

Nothing to see here. But, oh, so much to listen to. Begun from nothing other than a love of *Hamilton: An American Musical*, by someone WHO HADN'T EVEN SEE THE SHOW YET, *The Hamilcast* has become a key part of the *Hamilton* community - *The Hamilcast* is even included in the official *Hamilton* app (a great way to stay abreast of the latest episode). Early episodes focused on Ron Chernow's biography and included guests also obsessed with *Hamilton*, but the podcast began to attract interviews with members of the original *Hamilton* Broadway cast - Seth Stewart was the first - and has taken off from there, with Lin-Manuel Miranda himself starring in several #Lintoberfest episodes (starting with #88). The mostly weekly podcast is up to #199 as of now.

But the best thing about *The Hamilcast* is its community. The host, Gillian Pensavalle, has created the best *Hamilton* community there is - The Hamilcast Peeps (essentially Gillian's followers). Peep meets happen all the time, all over the place, and the community is incredibly welcoming and supportive, all starting from Gillian - she is simply a star. Not a day goes by that I don't check in on the group on social media (thehamilcast on all the things).

THE ALEXANDER HAMILTON AWARENESS SOCIETY

The Alexander Hamilton Awareness Society (AHA Society), established in 2011, has a stated purpose of increasing the awareness of and appreciation for Alexander Hamilton.

The AHA Society is a tremendous resource for scholarship about Hamilton, and they regularly give (and host) presentations and consult on, curate and contribute to exhibitions. They also host a program of annual events for several days around the anniversaries of each of Hamilton's birthday (January 11th) and the Hamilton-Burr duel (July 11th). The AHA Society is also an official partner to Hamilton Grange National Memorial, and many of these events are held there.

In addition to the activities and scholarship hosted by the AHA Society, they maintain a website - theAHAsociety.org - that has compiled a tremendous amount of information about Hamilton and is a great resource.

The AHA Society is a 501(c)(3) nonprofit, and you can support the organization by becoming a member.

CHAPTER ELEVEN

SUGGESTED ITINERARIES

Look around, look around...

Now that you know where everything is, you need to figure out what you really want to see and whether you have time to see it. I have included some suggestions on the following pages, organized by the amount of time required (Half-Day or Full-Day+). I have also included a couple of themed itineraries.

If you are planning a New York city trip far enough in advance, you should think about booking a tour with Jimmy Napoli, who is a rock star when it comes to talking about Alexander Hamilton's life in New York City (he's been giving Hamilton tours for 20 years) – he has a couple of different tours and you can book him through hamiltonsnewyork.com.

Downtown

A great place to start is (1) *Trinity Church* (page 29), where you can visit Alexander Hamilton's grave, as well as those of Eliza Hamilton and some others. A short walk down Wall Street from there takes you to (2) *Federal Hall* (page 25), and further down the block is (3) the *Museum of American Finance* (page 49), where you can see replicas of the Hamilton-Burr duel pistols and other Hamilton-related items (and where you can pick up a Hamilton tie in the gift shop). If you have time for lunch or a drink, you can head to (4) *Stone Street* (page 35), which has several restaurants, or (5) *Fraunces Tavern* (page 13). If you don't, you can walk the half-mile to (7) *the Common* (page 15) for a beautiful green spot to take a break (don't miss the stone inlay at the southern end of the park), swinging by (6) *Jefferson's Residence* (page 23) to see the commemorative plaque there on the way.

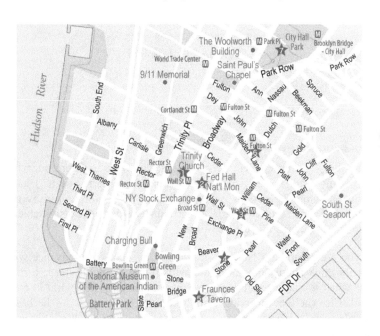

If you have some extra time, you can head to *Bayard's Mansion* (page 31) (either on your way downtown or on your way back uptown), to see the plaque commemorating where Hamilton was taken after the duel with Burr and where he died. The mansion is just over a quarter-mile walk from the subway station.

Daddy said not to go downtown...

Uptown

Start at (1) *the Grange* (page 27), and expect to spend at least two hours there if you go on a tour (either ranger-led or self-guided). Try to take a walk around the grounds if you have time – it can get crowded but is still quite peaceful. You can then swing by (2) St. Luke's Episcopal Church to see a statue of Alexander Hamilton (the Grange was acquired by the church in the late 1800s and temporarily moved to the grounds) and then head over to (3) *Morris-Jumel Mansion* (page 39), which is either a 1.1 mile walk or a 10-15 minute bus ride (walk over to St. Nicholas Avenue and take the M3 uptown – you can use your Metrocard). If you are interested in a tour, visit morrisjumel.org for a schedule – there are only about a half-dozen docent-led tours per month.

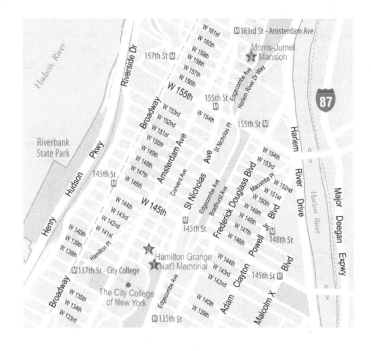

If you have time, head over to the 157th Street subway station to take the 1 train downtown to 116th Street, where you can visit the campus of Columbia University – *King's College* (page 19) is now Columbia College. There you can see a statue of Alexander Hamilton in front of Hamilton Hall.

It's quiet uptown...

Central Park Area

Start at (1) the *New-York Historical Society* (page 50), where you can see statues depicting the Hamilton-Burr duel, as well as several other Hamilton artifacts (the museum also houses artifacts and documents from the collection of the Gilder Lehrman Institute of American History, including a copy of the Reynolds Pamphlet – note that these documents are not on permanent display). The museum also held a Summer of Hamilton exhibit in the summer of 2016, with special Hamilton-related exhibits and events (hopefully this will become an annual event). If the weather is nice, take a walk across Central Park (three-quarters of a mile) to see (2) the statue of Alexander Hamilton (the statue was donated to the park in 1880 by Hamilton's son, John). From there you can head another mile uptown to (3) the *Museum of the City of New York* (page 52), where you can see portraits of Revolution-era historical figures, including Hamilton and George Washington. If it's a nice day and you have time, head over to (4) the Conservatory Garden (enter between 104th/105th Streets; open 8AM to dusk) - no connection with Hamilton, but a beautiful garden to take a walk through (while listening to *Hamilton*?).

Hamilton's Final Hours

Start in **Weehawken, NJ** (page 55), where Aaron Burr mortally wounded Alexander Hamilton during their duel on July 11, 1804. From there head to **Bayard's Mansion** (page 31), where Hamilton was taken following the duel and where he died the following day (with Eliza and Angelica at his side).

His funeral procession and burial were two days later, on July 14th. To follow the path of the procession, start from (1) the home of John and Angelica Church (Schuyler) and walk over to (2) **the Common** (page 15). The procession then wound along Beekman Street and down Pearl Street, taking you near (3) **Stone Street** (page 35), where Hamilton once had an office, and past (4) **Fraunces Tavern** (page 13) – either location would be a good place to stop for a drink or a meal if you need a break. Finally, head up Whitehall Street, going past the former site of (5) Fort George in **the Battery** (page 17) and then up Broadway past (6) **26 Broadway** (page 33), where Hamilton once lived, to (7) **Trinity Church** (page 29), where Hamilton was eulogized and laid to rest (and where you can pay your respects to Hamilton, among others).

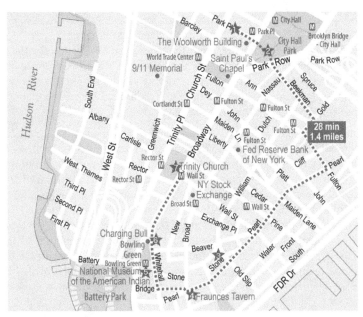

Unless you rush through it, this itinerary will take most of a day, so you may want to skip Weehawken if you only have half a day.

I hear wailing in the streets...

If You're More of a Burr Fan

This itinerary will take you all over the city and will require a full day unless you skip some portions (I've grouped together the locations that are near each other (Uptown, Downtown, SoHo and New Jersey) – skip an entire group if you're pressed for time). Since this itinerary covers so much area, I decided not to include a map – go to the individual pages for location information. Note that Federal Hall is closed Saturdays (except during the Summer) and Sundays and that Morris-Jumel Mansion is closed Mondays.

Start in New Jersey, at **Weehawken** (page 55), the site of Aaron Burr's famous duel with Alexander Hamilton (which branded Burr as *the villain in your history…*).

Next head Downtown, where Burr and Hamilton saw action in the American Revolution. Start at **Federal Hall** (page 25), where Burr and Hamilton defended Levi Weeks, then head over to **Fraunces Tavern** (page 13). Don't forget to make a reservation (see page 13) if you want to have lunch there. Take the half-mile walk up to **the Common** (page 15) to burn off some of your lunch.

Now go Uptown to **Morris-Jumel Mansion** (page 39). The easiest way to get there is to take the C train from Chambers Street uptown to 163rd Street, but if you're familiar with the subway it's faster to take the A train and then switch to the C (or the 2/3 uptown from Park Place and switch to the 1 train). Going here next may seem a bit out of order, but you need to get there and have time to look around before the mansion closes at 4PM (or 5PM on the weekends).

Finally, head down to SoHo for a couple of quick site visits. You can either take the 1 train from 157th Street downtown to Houston Street or the C train from 163rd Street downtown to Spring Street. Walk through the Charlton-King-Vandam Historic District, where the **Richmond Hill** (page 21) estate was once located (though there's nothing specific to see other than the Federal-style row houses that are now there). Now walk west to finish your day at the **COS Clothing Store** (page 51). In the basement of the store is the haunted well where the murder victim in the Levi Weeks trial was found. Not only was Burr part of the defense team for the trial, but the well was located on land owned by the Manhattan Company, which was founded by Burr as a bank to compete with Hamilton's Bank of New York.

If you're feeling really adventurous (and have the time), you can head down to Princeton Cemetery to visit Burr's grave.

I'm willing to wait for it…

All of the numbered sites in the Philadelphia map below are within a mile of each other, so travel time is not an issue. The determining factors in the number of sites you can visit in a half-day are the crowds, the amount of time you spend at each site and whether you include a meal at (11) *City Tavern* (page 81) in your visit. Each of (1) the *National Constitution Center* (page 88) (5) *Independence Hall* (page 67) and (10) the *Museum of the American Revolution* (page 87) requires more than an hour to properly see, so you can likely not visit more than two of them in a half-day (and maybe only one if you go to City Tavern). During heavy tourist season, the biggest lines tend to be at Independence Hall, so you may want to start or end there (and keep in mind that each of (3) the *Great Essentials Exhibit*, (4) *Congress Hall* (page 75) and (6) *Old City Hall* (page 73) are part of the Independence Hall complex and are accessed through the same security entrance), especially during the summer, when Independence Hall stays open late. Each of (9) the *First Bank of the United States* (page 71), (12) the *Treasury Office* (page 77) and (13) *Hamilton's Residence* (page 79) are just sites to see and don't really take any time to see.

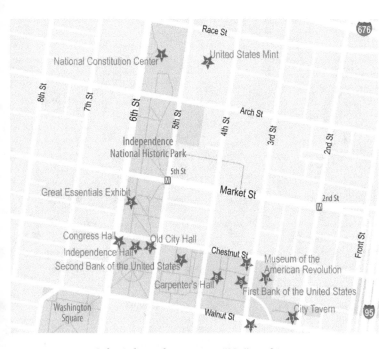

I don't know how to say "No" to this…

Unlike Philadelphia, the sites in Washington, D.C. are quite far apart - just to walk from (1) *Lafayette Square* (page 110) to (9) the *Library of Congress* (page 108) is more than two miles. Also, unless you have planned in advance, you won't be able to visit (2) the *White House* (page 97) or (3) the *Treasury Building* (page 101) as both of these required advance reservations (and if you are visiting one or both of those sites, you'll have to plan your itinerary around those tour times). In theory you could visit each of (5) the *National Portrait Gallery* (page 105) (6) the *National Archives Building* (page 106) (7) the *National Gallery of Art* (page 107)and (8) the *United States Capitol* (page 95) within a half-day, especially if you just focus on the Hamilton-related points, but each can easily occupy more than an hour of your time. Throw in lunch or dinner at (4) *The Hamilton*, and you probably only have time for a couple of those sites.

You can also combine a visit to the *Anderson House* (page 103, not on the map), but that probably means a trip on the Metro (and if you make the effort to get there, you probably want to take one of their excellent tours and spend some time there).

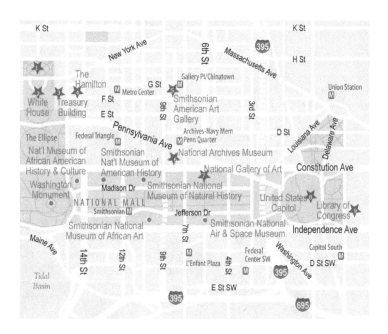

A trip to *Mount Vernon* (page 121) can also be done in a half-day, but probably only if you're driving (or take a car).

Well I propose the Potomac...

If you have one or more full days, you can start to think about seeing almost everything in NYC, Philly or D.C. or even heading out of the cities. Each bullet point below should take about a day, so combine them if you have more time and want to see more.

• **Combinations of Half-Day Itineraries**

You can combine any two of the NYC half-day itineraries (pages 137-139). Note that the Central Park itinerary leaves you on the Upper East Side, so if you're going to combine this with the Uptown itinerary, start with Uptown. You can also see more sites in Philadelphia (page 142) or D.C. (page 143).

• **Themed Itineraries**

You time for either NYC themed itineraries (pages 140 and 141), including a break to eat at *Fraunces Tavern* (page 13).

• **Farther Afield in New Jersey**

Consider visiting *Morristown* (page 57), *Elizabethtown* (page 61), *Paterson* (page 63), or the *Battle of Monmouth* (page 59).

Morristown – The train to Morristown takes about 80 minutes (each way, to/from NY Penn Station – see page 57 for details).

Elizabethtown – The train to Elizabeth takes about 30 minutes (each way, to/from NY Penn Station – see page 61 for details).

Paterson – The bus to Paterson takes about 45 minutes (each way, to and from NY Port Authority – see page 63 for details).

Battle of Monmouth – Monmouth Battlefield State Park is about a 70-80 minute drive (each way, from Times Square). If you're not driving, it will take about 2-1/2 hours to get there by bus (from Port Authority) and walking (this includes a 1.3 mile walk from the bus stop in New Jersey (the Freehold Raceway Mall stop), so assume more time if you're a slow walker).

• **Farther Afield in Virginia**

Yorktown – Yorktown is about a 2-1/2 to 3-hour drive from DC (each way, to/from DC Union Station – see page 117 for details). Williamsburg is only a 30-minute drive away.

Williamsburg – Williamsburg is about a 2-1/2 to 3-hour drive from DC (each way, to/from DC Union Station – see page 119 for details). Yorktown is only a 30-minute drive away.

Monticello – Monticello is about a 2-1/2-hour drive from DC (each way, to/from DC Union Station – see page 123 for details).

ACKNOWLEDGEMENTS

First and foremost, the inspiration for this book was clearly *Hamilton: An American Musical.* While credit for the show goes mainly to Lin-Manuel Miranda, I think that the show is also made by the incredibly talented men and women that perform the show every night (consider that as of the time I wrote the original edition of this book, I had seen the show twice and had not seen Miranda perform, and it was still the best show I'd ever seen; fortunately my daughter and I were finally able to see Miranda reprise the role of Hamilton in Puerto Rico in January 2019). Standouts for me are Leslie Odom, Jr., Daveed Diggs, Christopher Jackson, Jonathan Groff, Phillipa Soo and Renee Elise Goldsberry. They have together created something wonderful – it's amazing to me that such a huge community has developed around the show, and that it has been able to bridge across so many different groups of people.

Second would be Ron Chernow, whose biography *Alexander Hamilton* opened my eyes about the connections between the show and the locations where the events took place. I initially tried to give attribution in the book wherever Chernow's book was the source of my info, but it didn't lay out well. But please note that much of the info in this book is based upon Chernow's biography.

Third is the Alexander Hamilton Awareness Society (AHA), with a special thanks to their former president, Rand Scholet. Scholet provided a final set of eyes to confirm the historical accuracy of the original edition of the book, and he was responsible for the addition of a few of the locations. AHA's support for my book, and their welcoming of me into the Hamilton community, have been especially gratifying. I would also like to thank Nicole Scholet, who helped with images, promotion and my web presence, and Leonard A. Zax, who was instrumental in getting Paterson, N.J. into the original edition.

I want to further thank Nicole Scholet for all of her work in connection with this expanded edition of the book. I realized near the completion of the original edition that many of the events depicted in the show took place outside of NY/NJ, but I didn't have the time (or the motivation) at that time to do further research and writing. Writing this expanded edition was a plan from that time, but it took much longer than I expected (mainly because of my day job and my obligations there). Nicole provided a tremendous amount of research for the expanded edition about the Philadelphia sites and many of the Virginia and other further afield locations. I can see that I would have saved a lot of time doing research had I met Nicole before finishing the original edition of the book, but better late than never. In addition to Nicole Scholet,

I also want to thank Kristianna Anderson, Margaret Elise Vander Woude and Nicola Macgregor, who provided images for the expanded edition, and special thanks to Margaret for doing a final proofread of the expanded edition of the book (and for adding some much-needed consistency, including bringing me into the present by deleting all my double spaces).

Most important are my family – my kids London and Andrew and especially my wife, Rebecca. Our collective enthusiasm about the show really fed my interest in this project and drove me to take it on. Without their support and encouragement I may have never started this book, and I definitely would never have finished it. I also want to thank my mother-in-law, Jean Couban, whose enthusiasm helped keep me going when I was down about my failed Kickstarter campaign for this book.

I want to thank each of Richard Brookhiser, Douglas Hamilton, Rand Scholet, Carol S. Ward and Leonard A. Zax for taking the time to provide reviews for the book cover. I especially appreciate the support of my various commercial partners, who took a chance and carried my book in their stores and shops, and want to give special thanks to the New-York Historical Society, PIQ Stores and the National Parks, each of which has purchased more than 500 books. Even though many of them no longer carry the book, their initial support was key to spurring initial book sales, and those that still carry my book are helping it continue to have visibility – without this continued support I may not have finished this expanded edition.

Finally I want to thank everyone who supported my book, from the few who supported the Kickstarter campaign (Erynn Albert, John Bode, Thad Bzomowski, Ryan Carey, David Cohn, Jean Couban, Lucas Deshouillers, Cindy Elder, Julien Gimbrere, Adam Greene, Trey Key, Ger Laffan, Mike Loos, Rob O'Connell, Marissa Tai and Jerry Walrath) to Topher Horn and David Montoya, who gave me needed advice about putting a book together, and to everyone that's taken the time to write a review about the book. And I want to throw shout outs to Gary Vaynerchuk (I don't know him but I took his message of hustling to heart in putting in the time and work to get this done), and to Jimmy Napoli, who has been nothing but supportive of my book and has helped me get it out there.

Thanks for everything – I couldn't have done this without you!

IMAGE CREDITS

All photographs included in this book were taken by me (using my iPhone 6-plus or X) except for the following photographs, drawings or paintings:

Cover, Alexander Hamilton - By John Trumbull [Public domain], via Wikimedia Commons

Page 13, Fraunces Tavern – By Jim Henderson (Own work) [Public domain], via Wikimedia Commons; cropped by B.L. Barreras

Page 21, Richmond Hill – By Charles Haynes Haswell; cropped by Beyond My Ken (talk) 20:39, 19 June 2011 (UTC) - NYPL Digital Gallery [Public domain]

Page 25, Federal Hall – Archibald Robertson's "View up Wall Street" w/City Hall - [Public domain], via Wikimedia Commons

Page 27, The Grange – By OH.F. Langmann [Public domain], via Wikimedia Commons

Page 39, Morris-Jumel Mansion – By Beyond My Ken (Own work) [GFDL (http://www.gnu.org/copyleft/fdl.html) or CC BY-SA 4.0-3.0-2.5-2.0-1.0 (http://creativecommons.org/licenses/by-sa/4.0-3.0-2.5-2.0-1.0)], via Wikimedia Commons

Page 43, The Public Theater – By Nicola Macgregor (Own work), with permission; cropped by B.L. Barreras

Page 55, Aaron-Burr Duel – By Illustrator not identified. From a painting by J. Mund. [Public domain], via Wikimedia Commons

Page 59, Battle of Monmouth – Emanuel Leutze painted Washington Rallying the Troops at Monmouth [Public domain], via Wikimedia Commons

Page 61, The Snyder Academy of Elizabethtown – By Nicole Scholet (Own work), the Alexander Hamilton Awareness Society, with permission; cropped by B.L. Barreras

Page 63, Paterson Great Falls – photographer unknown, from the collection of Leonard A. Zax, with permission

SOURCE CREDITS

As mentioned under "Acknowledgements," I initially tried to include source attributions throughout the book, but it didn't really fit well with the book layout (and this is more of a tour guidebook than a history book, though I did spend a lot of time getting the history part correct). So rather than fact-by-fact attribution, I would like to instead recognize the sources used for this book.

First and foremost is Ron Chernow's *Alexander Hamilton* biography, which provided a lot of date information necessary to tie the events depicted in *Hamilton: An American Musical* to the locations where they occurred.

The timing of publication of *Hamilton: The Revolution*, by Lin-Manuel Miranda and Jeremy McCarter was fortuitous, as it helped me confirm some of the setting info for the show. And I very much enjoyed *Duel with the Devil: The True Story of How Alexander Hamilton and Aaron Burr Teamed Up to Take on America's First Sensational Murder Mystery*, by Paul Collins – while this did not provide much information for this book, it was key in sparking my intrigue about where events from Hamilton's life happened (since the trial occurred at Federal Hall, which had previously been the seat of the federal government).

Beyond these books, my research was done online and onsite. Where I provided information about visiting a location, I tried to get this information from the actual location (e.g., pamphlets or displays) for the New York City, New Jersey, Philadelphia and Washington, D.C. locations or directly from the website for the location (and I similarly tried to take historical information directly from that location or website, though this was often not provided). I also tried where possible to verify information that I obtained online against Chernow's book. The images other than my own photographs, photographs from friends and those provided by the Alexander Hamilton Awareness Society were all obtained through Wikipedia, primarily because it was the most direct source of public domain images (due to the site's own guidelines for posting images on the site).

Further descriptions and photographs for many of these sites can be found at AllPlacesHamilton.com. For recent and future events at Alexander Hamilton locations, in addition to many of the sites included in this book visit theAHAsociety.org. Both websites are provided by the Alexander Hamilton Awareness Society.

INDEX

INDEX BY SONG TITLE

ACT II

ABOUT BRYAN

Where Was the Room Where It Happened?: The Unofficial Hamilton - An American Musical *Location Guide* was self-published in 2016 and was Bryan's first foray into writing. He quickly followed it with his second Unofficial Location Guide, which was themed around *Fantastic Beasts and Where to Find Them. Where Was the Room Where It Happened?* is now being carried in retail locations around New York City, as well as some locations in New Jersey and Philadelphia, and it is available online where books are sold, in both ebook and paperback versions.

This is an expanded edition of the book, to add several locations tied to *Hamilton* that were not included in the original version (mainly because Bryan didn't realize how many of the events from the show occurred outside of New York until late in the process of writing the original version).

Bryan started his career as a mechanical engineer in Houston, TX, and relocated to Manhattan to attend law school at NYU. He has spent most of the past 25 years as a lawyer in New York City, though he has taken breaks both from being a lawyer and from living in New York (spending two years abroad, in London and Frankfurt). He lives on the Upper West Side in Manhattan with his wife of 27 years, his two kids and their Jack Russell terrier.

Follow Bryan on the following social media:

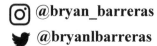 **@bryan_barreras**
@bryanlbarreras

ABOUT NICOLE

Nicole Scholet is a historian and public speaker on the founding period of the US, with a focus on the lives of Alexander Hamilton and Elizabeth Schuyler Hamilton.

Nicole serves as President of the Alexander Hamilton Awareness Society (AHA), a national nonprofit educational organization which provides extensive online resources, leads programs at historic locations, supports and presents historically accurate research about Hamilton's life and legacy, and serves as the official partner to the Hamilton Grange National Memorial.

Nicole's research has been used by various authors, museums, and historical societies, and is also shared through public speaking engagements. Additional professional experience includes The Colonial Dames of America, the Historical Society of Newburgh Bay and the Highlands, and Herzog and Co.

For more about Nicole's research and talks: nicolescholet.com

For more about the AHA Society: theAHAsociety.org.

ORDERING CUSTOM GUIDES AND EBOOK

Additional guides can be ordered online (Amazon or B&N) or purchased at retail locations (wwtrwih.com has a list of locations). Email me at Info@wwtrwih.com for bulk orders or to carry the book in your store. The book can also be customized (with your company color and/or logo on the cover, and customized text on the back cover) for corporate gifts - email me at Info@wwtrwih.com for further information.

This book is also available as an eBook on Amazon. The eBook has hyper-links to navigate you through the book (and to external websites), as well as zoomable fonts, maps and pictures.

THANKS SO MUCH FOR READING MY BOOK!

 @wwtrwih

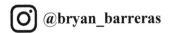 @bryan_barreras

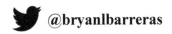 @bryanlbarreras